Mayors, Madams, and Madmen

Mayors, Madams, and Madmen

by Norman Mark

CHICAGO REVIEW PRESS • CHICAGO

First Edition
First Printing

Published by Chicago Review Press, Inc.
215 West Ohio Street, Chicago, Illinois 60610

ISBN: Paper 0-914090-70-4, Cloth 0-914090-69-0
Library of Congress Catalog Number : 79-554-86

Contents

Acknowledgements

If Herman Kogan hadn't written his books about Chicago, this one would never have been born. Emmett Dedmon and his wife spent months in the Chicago Historical Society painstakingly typing out notes for his book, *Fabulous Chicago*. Dedmon and Kogan, as Chicago Sun-Times archivist, allowed me to enter semi-secret rooms in that newspaper to see Dedmon's notes (and the Field Enterprises librarians, despite several moments of consternation, turned their backs most of the time when the Furtive Xeroxer emerged from the archives with Dedmon's notes).

The late John W. Clark, the Nighthawk, kept decades of scrapbooks when he was a tour guide in Chicago. His wife, the indomitable Margaret, turned 24 cases of them over to me. Clark was an incredible lover of his city and a man with the single-minded purpose of knowing his town.

Kenan Heise, editor of the Chicago Tribune's Action Line, is a collector of old books on Chicago, a friendly and accurate story-teller (a rarity), the best after-midnight coffee maker in town, a man who enjoys correcting manuscripts, and a man who enjoyed selling his books to me. If I now own more than half a library of Chicago historical books, it is because Heise loved each one and was willing to part with it for the right price.

There were many more men and women, whom I met only through their books and who deserve thanks. Herbert Asbury's *Gem of the Prairie* is an excellent, often hilarious look at Chicago's underworld. Kogan and Lloyd Wendt's *Lords of the Levee* brings to life two of Chicago's most colorful crooked aldermen. William T. Stead's *If Christ Came to Chicago* (1894, but reissued by Heise and John Perri in 1979) can make contemporary readers angry. Lloyd Lewis and Henry Justin Smith gave the city an accurate word poem in *Chicago, The History of Its Reputation,* while Finis Farr was delightfully nasty in his history *Chicago.* And no new book about Chicago's past could be written without intimately knowing the exquisitely boring and sometimes delightful three-volume *History of Chicago* (1885), by A. T. Andreas, which my neighbor Kathy Hogan found, leather-bound, in her basement and was kind enough to loan to me. Contemporary readers shuld also make note of Bessie Louise Pierce's detailed three-volume *History of Chicago.*

This book owes much to the suggestions of my former agent (and current publisher) Arthur F. Gould and to my publisher Curt Matthews. Their not-so-casual suggestion at a Christmas party two years ago resulted in more work than either they predicted or their advance paid for.

Finally, my sincere thanks to my children, Geoffrey and Joel, who stayed out of the room with all the dusty, falling-apart books for endless months, and to my wife, Rhoda, who understood each time I said I stayed up all night with a whore from the 1880s.

Norman Mark August, 1979 Chicago, Ill.

Introduction

What stories would movers and shakers of Chicago's past tell if they could sit around a cracker-barrel or at a long bar stocked with fine whiskey and try to top each other with their best tales?

They certainly would not talk about numbers of hogs slaughtered or population statistics, wars won, parades held or vote totals. And yet their stories might more accurately reflect what should be remembered about creating a city out of a mud lake.

A city's past only barely exists. The present will often tear it down and replace it with glass-and-steel antiseptic boxes.

The past is gone. Faded. Forgotten. Or made dull and clean.

But the stories can be found and remembered.

And Chicago's stories prove that it was, is and perhaps always will be a frontier town celebrating rude, fast, loud, sweaty pleasures. A city which will give power, wealth and fame to those who would grab it. And a city which demands a dollar's return for a dollar's bribe.

Many of the most memorable legends-of-truth demonstrate that Chicago was corrupt from the moment it rose from the ooze. I suspect it may always be the payoff capitol of the world. The bribe is fast, easy and cheap. It usually gets results.

INTRODUCTION

Revealed thievery is hated, locally. Hated, that is, on the day it is discovered. About 20 years later, the outrageous thief, swindler or corrupt city official often becomes someone quaint, a person subject to local nostalgia.

Chicago is a town with an absolute double standard. Getting caught is worse than stealing. It shows your amateur status. And Chicagoans, despite their decades' long support of the perpetually losing Cubs, hate amateurs.

Chicagoans very secretly admire their home-grown crooks and gangsters. The town might never have a payoff museum, where tourists might see envelopes stuffed with bribes thrust into the jacket pockets of performers on the hour throughout the afternoon—that would be too public. The town never saved the wall against which stood the men murdered during the St. Valentine's Day Massacre, even though tourists would pay to see it. But the town sure doesn't mind remembering when Grandpa bought home brew from the bootleggers and, by golly, do you remember the time when he looked Al Capone right in the eye and told him to mind his own business and keep his hands off grandma? That had never happened to Capone before, but Scarface (that's what gramps called him, you know) backed down and admired Grandpa, yes he did.

Chicagoans boast about their lakefront, their garbage collection and the fact that the city somehow still works, after lurching through the '60s and '70s.

But it works, and is unique, as much because of the church-going, money-saving, lawn-cutting, one-

marriage-in-a-lifetime folks as because of the gun-
toting, bribe-giving-and-taking, swaggering, bragging,
whoring, gambling people.

This book is simply a collection of stories which
deserve retelling because they still hold the power to
fascinate. Everyone you'll meet had the energy to seek
their sometimes strange goals, the single-minded
purpose of affecting their contemporaries and the luck
to gain verbal and written immortality.

It is a book dedicated to the city on the lake, make
and take.

Chapter One: The Madams

"If it weren't for married men,
we couldn't have carried on at
all and if it weren't for
cheating married women, we could
have made another million."
        The Everleigh Sisters circa 1910

It's a pity that Chicago's madams and harlots seldom wrote about what they did, because they were—and are—a most energetic lot.

Herbert Asbury's *Gem of the Prairie* estimates that Chicago's 5000 prostitutes in 1911 had 27,375,000 assignations. The figures are only an approximation. It certainly could have been higher than that.

Chicago's entire population was 2,250,000 at the time, suggesting that every man, woman and child in the city had 12 meetings with prostitutes per year, or one a month. If women and children, plus aged, infirm and senile men, are eliminated from the figure, one can see how active both the male and female populations of the city were. (Of course, there were many out-of-town visitors that year, a fact which would decrease the local average.)

The activities of two local chippies, Kitty and Florince, reveal what a busy life they led. On a single Thursday, Florince entertained 45 men (!), many more

1

than the 21 each who enjoyed her charms on the previous Tuesday and Wednesday. On Sunday, a day off for most people, Florince saw 20 men, while Kitty embraced 24. The average per day was 26 men for Florince and 15 for Kitty. Florince's profits for seeing 130 men in five days was $32.50. Obviously, Florince was not in the business for the money alone.

In 1857, an inmate of one whore house died and the coroner was told she had neither been sober nor out of the house for five years and had not worn a stitch of clothing for three years. The verdict: She died of "intemperance."

One Chicago whore house had a few uncut books and was called The Library. Another featured light-skinned Negro girls for white men, plus "bestial circuses." Another had Japanese and yet another had Chinese women for white men. Rumor had it that these Oriental women, who suffered during the long, cold Chicago winters, would ply their trade while dressed in long woolen underwear or fur coats.

The House of All Nations had a $5 and a $2 entrance. When business was brisk at one doorway, the $2 girls would cross the house and be transformed into $5 girls.

Any act imagined in the 20th century—men and men, women and women, women and animals, group sex, female impersonators—was available for sale in 19th century Chicago.

Chicago tried now and then to control its prostitutes, but the town wavered between seeing hookers as a necessary evil (the theory was that they prevented rapes, calmed the savagery of local males and were good for convention business) and trying unsuccessfully to eliminate them for moral reasons. In 1835, when the population was less than 4,000, an ordinance was passed fining owners of brothels $25. In 1838, with the population at 4,273, the fine was increased.

The most stylish whore houses were the scenes of the best stories, but that does not mean that prostitution in Chicago was ever completely romantic or gentle. It was seamy and rough. It regularly exploited women, and men.

There were white slavers in Chicago who would import teen-aged girls and sell them to brothels. One girl, after being kept a prisoner in a whore house for six months in 1907, told police that she was taken there and "my street clothes were taken away from me, and there was nothing for me to do but to submit to orders . . . I stayed there until I thought I should go mad if I could not escape." One stockade just outside Chicago kept women behind bars until they were ready to be sold. Another gang specialized in selling Russian Jewesses, who were particularly favored in local whore houses. They were stripped, raped, inspected and sold to the highest bidders. One 18-year-old girl said she had been drugged and continuously raped for three days, after which she was sold for $50. And this was in 1907, more than 40 years after slavery was outlawed in America.

Although what you are about to read might, at times, sound luxurious and light-hearted, remember that in addition to the best houses there were the cribs where drugged, drunken women plied their trade.

THE TOUGHEST WHORE IN CHICAGO

Mother Conley sold rotten apples on street corners. Her husband owned a "miserable cart and an apology for a knock-kneed, one-eyed, suffering animal once believed to be a horse." Together they saved their money and bought what came to be known in the 1850s as Conley's Patch, in the near west side of the city. Here the dregs lived.

The most famous and feared denizen of Conley's Patch was known as the Bengal Tigress, who found young girls for sailors. She was so big and so powerful that her rare arrests took the combined strengths of no fewer than four of Chicago's finest, and even then they weren't sure of accomplishing their mission. She had to be literally dragged to the police station because no patrol wagons existed. (One crook was taken to prison in a wheelbarrow.)

When the Bengal Tigress had her dander up, beware. She was known to have chased more than one Conley's Patch resident into his or her home and then, after the door was bolted, to have torn down the entire shanty with her bare hands!

THE BEST FIGHT PURSE IN TOWN

By the late 1850s, Mother Herrick became famous for expanding the treats in store for her customers. Herbert Asbury in *Gem of the Prairie* revealed that in addition to providing dancing every night and an erotic show once a week, her house featured a monthly, bare-knuckle fist fight. The battlers would win $2 and a night with one of Mother Herrick's boarders.

Mother Herrick's place was finally raided, but not for prostitution, dancing or sex shows. It was closed because the prize fighting had to be stopped.

WHY NOT?

Roger Plant had a unique way of advertising his whoremongering. His den of iniquity, which flourished during the Civil War, was called Under the Willows. As the war continued, Roger Plant prospered and bought ever more adjoining buildings until his whore house was a half a block long.

It had many windows. On each window there was a bright blue shade. And on each shade was the question —and the advertisement—"WHY NOT?"

Roger Plant weighed only 100 pounds and was less than five feet one inch tall, but he was a fearsome fighter with knives, pistols or teeth. His wife, who weighed 250 pounds, could easily tame him by holding him at arm's length with one hand and spanking him with the other, according to Herbert Asbury.

This odd couple had about 15 children (estimates vary). Then daddy went straight.

After the Civil War, Roger Plant closed down Under the Willows to become a gentleman farmer. He said, "The country life was best for the children." Not quite.

Roger Jr. owned three saloons and two bordellos. Two of the Plants' daughters went into the whoremongering business. One of them, Kitty Plant, became famous locally for her shows featuring ladies and live stock. Ah! the country life.

THE MILLIONAIRE STREETWALKER

By 1877, Frances Warren, also known as Waterford Jack, had achieved her reputation as Chicago's "millionaire streetwalker." She once boasted that, during the previous decade, neither rain, nor snow, nor sleet of night halted her on her self-appointed rounds. Every night, 365 days a year, she worked, entertaining from five to 20 men for from $1 to $10 each.

A local newspaper took note of her in 1877, commenting, "Waterford Jack has $22,000 in the bank, every cent of which she had picked up on the streets of Chicago . . . It is said to her credit that she never stole a cent and was never drunk in her life. She is a pug-nosed, ugly-looking little critter, but for all that she has prospered in her wretched business and now stands before the world the richest street-walker in existence."

Others would earn more than Waterford Jack, but her life reminds us that perseverance, grit and determination can pay off. She was the Horatio Alger of prostitutes.

WHAT MORE COULD BE EXPECTED OF A GOOD WOMAN?

After 1871, Carrie Watson paid more property taxes on her coach and horses than did men named Field, Pullman and McCormick.

Legend has it that Carrie Watson arrived in Chicago at age 18, a virgin, a condition which did not last for long. After examining the professions available to a girl with looks and intelligence and rejecting being a shop girl, she spent two years as an apprentice whore in Lou Harper's establishment. Then she went into business for herself and became the capitalist success story of local whoredom.

By 1873, she was the owner and operator of the finest bordello in America, with 20 bedrooms, a billiard room and bowling alley, upholstered damask furniture, walls festooned with paintings and tapestries, three-piece orchestras playing day and night, and as many as 60 young ladies of the evening in residence.

Wine was served in silver buckets. The ladies made love on the purest linen sheets.

Those who entered her house never forgot the experience. In 1889, the Sporting & Club House Directory positively glowed when it described the joys of Ms. Watson's place:

441 S. Clark Street . . . 20 boarders, rates $5 to $50; pool rooms, billiard rooms, wine and beer. In fact, everything and plenty of it. This is one of the most widely known 'sporting' houses in the United States or Canada. Nothing west of the Alleghenys begins to compare with it in brilliance or magnificence. In the basement are the billiard and pool rooms with perfect appointments. On the first floor are five parlors and a music room (in the latter of which competent musicians are constantly in attendance) and these parlors defy description . . . A moment in the brilliantly lighted corridor, resplendent with bronze and crystal decora-

tions, and one is ushered into the far and justly famed 'Mikado' parlor with its four walls and ceiling composed of solid French plate mirrors . . . The English language is inadequate to describe the feeling of one who enters this enchanted bower for the first time . . . The hand that writes this grows palsied at the recollection and these lines if longer drawn out will end in an inky blur . . . Miss Watson's is THE HOUSE of the West, and as such should be the Mecca of all male tourists. Her boarders are of such variety that any taste is sure to be suited and no living human being ever went away from the house dissatisfied.

It was some whore house!

There were no tacky red lights outside this house. No ladies sat in the windows beckoning to the trade. Instead, there was a famous parrot in an outside cage, saying over and over again, "Carrie Watson. Come in Gentlemen."

The parrot retired with Ms. Watson when she left the business and rumor has it the bird was later given to Bathhouse John Coughlin, famous boodling alderman, when he decided to create his own zoo (see Chapter Three on politicians for that story).

William T. Stead, a crusader who shocked the city with his 1894 book *If Christ Came to Chicago*, was angered by Ms. Watson's trade, but praised her nonetheless. He noted, "Carrie Watson is a smart woman, said to be liberal in her gifts to the only churches in her neighborhood, one a Catholic just across the way and the other a Jewish synagogue which local rumor asserts is run rent free owing to Carrie's pious munificence.

This is probably a slander, but its circulation is significant as proving that Carrie Watson can be all things to all men."

As befitting someone who had made a success of herself, Carrie Watson dressed in silk, wore diamonds, had two snow-white carriages with bright yellow wheels, and a coachman in scarlet livery.

The Sporting Life Newspaper noted, "Miss Carrie Watson says she would be willing to reform, but she can't think of anything she has been guilty of. She charges regular prices for wine, never cheated a man or a woman out of a cent, never told a lie, never starved her boarders, never got drunk, and never even took as much as a pinch of snuff." Now what more could be expected of a good woman?

On Teaching Girls the Value of a Good Home

From all accounts, Vina Fields was the Girl Scout of madams. She ran a huge brothel, normally inhabited by more than 40 boarders, with twice that number during the 1893 World's Fair. Her place specialized in black girls for a white clientele. In tribute to her, it was said that she never bribed a policeman, she was never raided and no complaints were ever heard against her.

Her rules were severe. No drunkenness. No nudity in the parlors and hallways. No hustling from the windows. Violators to be banished from the premises.

The rules "could hardly be more strict if they were drawn up for the regulation of a Sunday school," according to Mr. Stead, who wanted to reform

Chicago, and who died aboard the *Titanic* in 1912. It is odd that much of what we know about Vina Fields is from a Christian opposed to prostitution, and that nearly everything Stead had to say about her was complimentary.

Stead noted that Vina Fields "is bringing up her daughter, who knows nothing of the life of her mother, in the virginal seclusion of a convent school, and she (Ms. Fields) contributes of her bounty to maintain her unfortunate sisters whose husbands down South are among the hosts of the unemployed. Nor is her bounty confined to her own family. Every day, this whole winter through, she had fed a hungry, ragged regiment of the out-of-works. The day before I called, 201 men had had free dinners of her own providing."

Stead advised the world to listen to the wisdom of this "colored keeper of a house of ill fame." In her letter to Stead, Vina Fields said prostitutes came from every stratum of society and she counseled, "These women are no more lustful than their sisters in other positions in life. They simply have not been successful in marrying a home and as many, very many, do not know how to do any kind of work, they come here."

She even had a solution to the problem, one which might be loathed by 20th Century liberated women. Vina Fields wrote, "The only remedy for prostitution will be to educate women in the value of home life."

Ms. Fields suggested that young women be

. . . taught by mother to believe that the grandest and best work of women is to be able to

produce a grand, noble woman or man; and that
to do this her home must be a heaven.

. . . The great cry of today is the advancement of
woman—that means for all to make a grand rush for
outside employment, other than home work. While the
husbands and sons are walking the streets idle, the
mothers and sisters are earning the living, and by so
doing, the homes from necessity are dirty and the
younger children uncared for or left with ignorant
nurses, and this state of affairs makes the women tired
and fretful. The husbands, when they have money,
naturally seek the house of ill-fame, as wives are too
tired from work or devoting their time to society, to
give husbands even a pleasant word. Yes, I say, the only
way out of this trouble is to teach girls the value of
home, and when women in a mass elevate their homes
and make them all that the word implies, that is, clean,
home-like and cheerful; their kitchen the cleanest and
most cheerful room in the house, and their parlor for
use of the family instead of strangers; the houses of ill-
fame will have to shut up shop. They will have to close
for want of patronage.

When this is made the highest ambition of a girl's life,
to be a possessor of a model home by her virtues; and
the boys, by the mother, are taught to value a good
woman; they will then think it an honor to keep those
homes clean and wear a bright smile for husband and
little ones, and will then know the value of a clean calico
dress, a gingham apron for work and a white apron for
the eyes of father and dear children. There is not a man

living that would not prefer a dear little home to a
'wandering, no-account, hap-hazard life.

Vina Fields would never join the National Organization of Women!

A WOMAN MADE TO BE PLUNDERED

Mary Hastings has a terrible reputation, despite the fact
that she once set an important legal precedent.

She arrived in Chicago in 1888, a veteran of brothels
in Brussels, Paris, Toronto, British Columbia, Denver,
Portland and San Francisco. And she was only in her
mid-twenties.

When she complained that the bribes she was forced
to pay to Chicago's police were too high ($2.50 per week
per beat patrolman, plus free booze, food and women),
a police captain shouted, "Why, damn you, what are
you made for but to be plundered?" It was the sort of
statement to make a lady edgy.

At the time, police would walk around armed with
"John Doe," "Jane Doe" or "Richard Roe" warrants.
They would then arrest anybody whose actions fit the
pre-written warrants. But a high court upheld Madam
Hastings' protests that such warrants were illegal. Thus
her efforts were instrumental in making the police
observe the law.

Later, three policemen bearing a grudge entered her
place of business and smashed her furniture. After
complaining to the Mayor, the three policemen and
their sergeant were fired.

All that would have made Madam Hastings something of a hero to history, except for the fact that she was a thoroughly disreputable harridan. She often boasted that no one could suggest an act so disgusting that it could not be performed in her Custom House establishment. Her boast was never proved untrue.

She also specialized in luring young girls, ages 13 to 17, to her place, where they were raped by six or more men before becoming prostitutes.

Girls in her establishment were awakened with a cocktail at noon, took absinthe for breakfast, sat in the windows rapping on the panes for customers and were relieved every quarter hour until dinner time. They were put to bed drunk around 5 a.m.

Describing Madam Hastings' girls (and others), one Chicago detective wrote,

The costumes worn by these people embraced every kind known to the human race, from that of the Hottentot to the belle of the ball. Some wore tights, some having nothing on but a loose Mother Hubbard, made of some flashy material which resembled a mosquito bar, through which the entire form of the woman could be seen. Others were dressed as jockeys, while others had no sleeves in their dresses. The waist was cut so low that their bosoms were entirely exposed, and some were dressed almost exclusively in the garb which nature gave them when they were born . . . . Many of these women were even lower than brutes . . . .

Among the worst characters on this street was Mary Hastings . . . (whose) women were compelled to commit crimes, and nearly every man who entered one of the (houses) was robbed before he got out.

Obviously, Mary Hastings didn't care about word-of-mouth business. One wonders why so many customers kept on coming back?

THE WOMAN THEY COULDN'T ARREST

"Panel houses" plagued Chicago for decades. In these brothels, the paneled rooms were furnished with only a bed and a chair. The man naturally put his pants on the chair before entering the bed and the prostitute. While he was pursuing amour (or whatever), a panel would open near the chair. The paneled walls hid both a secret room and another girl who was adept at removing wallets from pants placed over chairs.

In 1896, $1,500,000 was stolen this way in Chicago.

One of the most successful owners of panel houses was Black Susan Winslow, who attempted to introduce automation to prostitution. Her girls would do anything to attract a man's attention—ring sheep bells or alarm clocks, hiss or tap on the windows. They finally created a mechanical woman whose hand automatically struck the window for them, beckoning passersby to enter.

There were so many complaints of robbery within Black Susan's establishment that Clifton R. Wooldridge was finally called upon. He was, according to his own book, *The World's Greatest Detective*, the Incorruptible Sherlock Holmes of America. In fact, he wrote of himself that "no braver, more honest or efficient police officer ever wore a star or carried a club." That was probably true. He made 19,500 arrests between 1888 and 1910, but Black Susan may have been his most difficult pinch.

She weighed 449 pounds. In fact she was so fat that she could no longer fit through any window or door of her establishment. Black Susan laughed and thought she was arrest-proof, according to Herbert Asbury's *Gem of the Prairie*. And she was, until Detective Wooldridge came upon the scene.

Wooldridge merely took the back door to her place off its hinges, sawed a two-foot section out of her wall, ran two 16-foot planks from the door-sill to his patrol wagon, unhitched one horse, tied a rope around Black Susan's waist, tied the other end to the horse's collar, and dragged her up the incline until she pleaded for mercy from the slivers which were festooning her ample behind. She went to jail, lying on her stomach as one of her girls removed the splinters.

DESERVED TO BE ROBBED

When ruling on a robbery which took place in Chicago's notorious Levee District, with more brothels per square block than any place else in town, Judge James Goggin said that any man who went into the Levee deserved to be robbed. He then set the thieves free!

THE MORALS CRUSADE THAT FLOPPED

On Oct. 18, 1909, Gypsy Smith, an evangelist, led thousands of people in a parade against the vice of the Levee, the notorious Chicago red light district.

The Salvation Army band played "Where Is My Wandering Boy Tonight," and then the throng knelt in the street and prayed.

At that moment, the Levee was silent. No red lights were on. No prostitutes were seen in the windows. No ragtime pianos played. No customers were knocking at the doors.

Alas, this crusade against vice, sex and smoking cigarettes was an abysmal failure. Many a young, pure man who followed Gypsy Smith into the Levee had never seen the place before. After Smith and most of the group left, the Levee reportedly had one of its most profitable nights ever as male purity yielded to siren temptations.

ANOTHER CRUSADE THAT FLOPPED
(THERE WERE MANY)

On Sept. 28, 1912, Virginia Brooks led 5,000 people into the Levee, accompanied by mounted police, Boy Scouts, Campfire Girls, floats depicting the evils of smoking (especially among Chicago Cubs' baseball players), students from the Garrett Biblical Institute and the Moody Bible Institute, girls from the Baptist Missionary Training School, children representing the Women's Christian Temperance Union, and a float with a banner saying that Norwegians would use Thor's hammer to smite the saloon-brothels.

Gypsy Smith's earlier foray into the Levee eventually led to the 1911 Vice Commission report, which helped close the Everleigh House (the Vice Commission report and the Everleigh House are both subjects of stories later in this chapter). Some say that Ms. Brooks forced the State's Attorney of Cook County reluctantly to raid the Levee. Arrest warrants were obtained for 135 keepers, owners and agents of property used for immoral purposes.

But that led to reprisals from the Levee. Big Jim Colosimo and others decided to strike back. They ordered all the harlots of Chicago to wear their loudest clothes and to go to "respectable neighborhoods" to ring doorbells and to ask for lodgings. The prostitutes were saying that segregated vice in one area of the city would be better than women selling their wares throughout the city.

But segregated vice ended. And almost immediately there were second thoughts on the matter. The Chicago Protective League for Women thought the campaign was a "monstrous mistake." Perhaps they were right. Prostitution didn't stop with the closing of the Levee. It just found other homes and other modes of existence.

THE OFFICIAL REPORT THEY COULDN'T MAIL

Even today, the 1911 Vice Commission Report, titled *The Social Evil in Chicago*, is very scandalous and quite racy.

It was ultimately shocking in 1911. In fact, shortly after the report was presented to Mayor Fred Busse, on April 5, 1911, the United States government barred it from the mails.

Mayor Busse had reluctantly agreed to create the

report and the City Council, which was never generous about learning what it didn't want to know, voted $5,050 to fund it. The report was ready after 98 special meetings of its commission.

The 1911 report was incredibly and frankly honest. A few excerpts are included so the reader can get the flavor of the original:

Page 29: "For the type of officer who frequents saloons and drinks openly with prostitutes, who acts as a guide to houses of assignation, and who recommends certain women for the purpose of prostitution—for this type of police officer Chicago has no place." (No further explanation of this entry is included. How many cops did that? Where? When? How often?)

Pages 34-35: Investigators looked at 445 saloons with 929 prostitutes and "were solicited by more than 236 women in 236 different saloons." (Did the investigators leave after only one woman solicited them? How attractive were the investigators?)

Page 44: After decrying the fact that the average shop girl earned only $6 a week in 1911, the report melodramatically asked, " . . . and with what does she meet? The advances of men without either a spark of bravery or honor, who hunt as their unlawful prey this impoverished girl, this defenseless child of poverty, unprotected, unloved and uncared for as she is plunged into the swirling, seething stream of humanity; the advances of men who are so low that they have lost even a sense of sportsmanship, and who seek as their game an underfed, a tired and a lonely girl."

Page 47: Prostitution is "a man and not a woman problem which we face today—commercialized by man —supported by man—the supply of fresh victims furnished by men—men who have lost the fine instinct of chivalry . . . "

Page 69: The report complained that the General Superintendent of Police twice gave the Commission a census of "disorderly resorts" in the city and twice it was "incomplete." As we shall later see, one famous house of ill-repute had an unlisted address in the police files!

Page 71: "Taking the number of women on the police lists alone . . . or 1,012, and multiplying that number by the average number of services daily, or 15 instances, or 15,180 daily, this makes a grand total of 5,540,700 (meetings with prostitutes in Chicago) per annum." Other sources figured there were at least 5,000 full time prostitutes, and thus arrived at the figure of 27,375,000 contacts per year.

Page 97: "One madame testified before the Commission that in a 50-cent house on the West Side, she with one girl took in $175 to $200 per week. She also testified that she herself entertained 60 men in one night at 50 cents each." The mind and possibly other parts of the body boggles.

Page 115: The report attempted to estimate the Chicago natives' contribution to prostitution. The population was about 2,000,000 at the time, with 400,000 families. The report assumed there would be two males (one father, one son) per family and the report allowed that there might be 800,000 local males available and attracted to the prostitute population. But then one must eliminate those infirm because of age, health, poverty or those unwilling because of religious influences. That left, the report estimated, only 200,000 local men available to be entertained by prostitutes, a population wholly unable to provide the estimated $5,400,000 per year flowing into local whore houses. The Commission then assumed that Chicago received 60,000 visitors per day, of which 20,000 were "eligible." They would be more than enough to assure the continuance of the $5,400,000 per year.

Page 126: A reference to a saloon on (X321) avenue (exact addresses weren't listed) where the entertainment was "men who impersonate females . . . Unless these men are known, it is difficult to detect their sex. They solicit men at the tables for drinks the same as women, and ask them to go upstairs for pervert practices."

Page 152: The infamous mention of the Everleigh House. "The (X523), at (X524, X524a) Dearborn Street. This is probably the most famous and luxurious house of prostitution in the country. The list received from the General Superintendent of Police on August 16, 1910, did not give the address of this house, nor of eleven other similar places on the street. The revised list received October 26th did mention the place, as well as others."

Page 155: "(X588) Wabash Avenue (not on police list). October 8th at 2:33 a.m. officer No. (X589) knocked on the side door of this saloon and was admitted. The officer seemed to be well known to the proprietor. When he came in, he went to the closet. Later the investigator saw him in the closet sitting on a box drinking a bottle of beer. At 2:40 a.m. another officer came in through the side door and joined the other officer in the closet." The closet must have been larger than most!

Page 156: A story which has been repeated in Chicago throughout its history—"(X615) Wabash Avenue (Not on police list). October 31st at 2:30 a.m. place was crowded at this hour, and several persons were intoxicated. Two strangers, who had the appearance of being farmers, were with two prostitutes. They complained to the waiter that he had overcharged them, and proceeded to argue with him about the right price of the drinks. They were ejected from the saloon. Later they returned with two officers, who called the waiter and spoke a few words to him.

"The officers then turned to the farmers and told them to 'beat it or they would be arrested.' The men appeared surprised, and finally left as one of the officers was about to hit one of them with his club. The two officers then entered the cafe, and holding their hands over their stars, went to the rear closet, took their uniform coats off, and put on ordinary coats, which were much too small for them. They then took off their helmets and sat down with the same prostitutes who had been drinking with the two farmers. They did not pay for their drinks."

Page 170: "This particular house has white girls who receive Chinamen only—no man of any other nationality is permitted to enter . . . "

Page 187: "Bessie, 20 years old, works in department

store. Salary $6 per week, and 'solicits' on the side. Left home on account of stepmother. Rooms with chum. Will go any place with fellows.

"Mag, 18 years old. Works in department store. Salary $5.50 per week. Tells parents she receives more. Helps support parent and 'solicits' at dances for spending money. Father is sickly."

Page 217: An investigation of excursion boats revealed, "Stateroom No. 74 was occupied by two girls and two young men; one of the girls was standing in front of the dressing table with nothing on except a dress skirt while the other called to a boy who happened to pass."

Page 250: An investigation of ice cream parlors noted, "Two girls and two boys were seen in this place after 10 p.m. The girls appeared to be from 15 to 16 years of age, the boys from 17 to 20. There was a Japanese screen in the room, which could be used to put around the tables. One of the boys took hold of the breast of one of the girls and took other liberties."

Among the Commission's recommendations was a suggestion for better sex education in the schools. The Commission concluded, "The honor of Chicago, the fathers and mothers of her children, the physical and moral integrity of the future generation demand that she repress public prostitution."

The city tried. Indeed, public prostitution was inconvenienced in a few places in Chicago. And that is about the most that can be demanded of any vice study ever made in Chicago.

THE FINEST WHORE HOUSE IN THE WORLD

The finest brothel ever created was no accident. It was the result of careful, painstaking research; the delicate application of the "build a better mousetrap" technique of merchandising, and the knowledge that the proprietors were the right people in the right place at the right time.

Minna and Ada Lester were born in Virginia in the 1870s. Their father was a wealthy lawyer who sent them to finishing school and who made sure that his daughters had society debuts. At least that's what the Lesters told their biographers.

They married brothers, but both these Southern gentlemen were cads. They quickly divorced the brothers and set off on a theatrical tour.

They invested their $35,000 inheritance, received when their father died, in a house of prostitution in Omaha, and doubled their money within a year.

They then did extensive research in Washington, New York, New Orleans and San Francisco, before settling on Chicago as the site of their next capitalistic venture.

They purchased a South Side brothel for $55,000 ($20,000 down payment, the remainder to be paid in six months, with $500 a month in rent). For their money, they got a lease, the fixtures and all the girls in the late Lizzie Allen's establishment. Minna and Ada fired the girls and threw away the fixtures, redecorating the house throughout.

The most famous brothel the world would ever know was ready to open on Feb. 1, 1900. The girls had already changed their names from Lester to Everleigh, from their grandmother's signature on letters ("Everly Yours") and as a tribute to Sir Walter Raleigh's poetry.

Descriptions of the sumptuous Everleigh House can still cause one to pause. Consider:

The Everleigh Club had an art gallery with good paintings, a dining room, a library, music room, ballroom and parlors with the titles Moorish, Gold, Silver, Copper, Red, Rose, Green, Blue, Oriental, Japanese, Egyptian, and Chinese. These rooms had knick-knacks, cushions, divans, sea shells, rugs and statues. Some had mirrors on the ceilings.

One girl had fresh cut roses everywhere with a Turkish mattress covered in white cashmere. Another girl enjoyed the color white and had an ermine coverlet on her bed. Every room had 18-karat gold cuspidors. (Heavyweight champ Jack Johnson opened a cafe about this time and he boasted that his gold spittoons were worth $57 each. The Everleigh Sisters sniffed, "The rims of ours cost more than that.")

The home was festooned with golden silk curtains, silk damask easy chairs, mahogany tables, gold bathtubs, gold-rimmed china and silver dinner ware, Irish linen and Spanish drawnwork tablecloths, and a gilded piano worth $15,000. Every room was equipped with a fountain which regularly jetted perfume into the air.

The Everleigh Club employed 15 to 25 of the finest chefs and maids in the nation. Breakfast, served at 2 p.m, might be iced clam juice, eggs Benedict, kidney saute, clam cakes with bacon, planked white fish, shad roe, breast of chicken with ham under glass, buttered toast supreme and Turkish coffee. The girls could have breakfast in their rooms. Dinner, at 8 p.m., might be supreme of guinea-fowl, pheasant, capon, roast turkey, duck and goose, quail on toast, au gratin cauliflower, spinach cups with creamed peas, parmesan potatoes, pear salad with sweet dressing, artichokes, stuffed cucumber salad, asparagus, candied and plain carrots, with fruit, pecans and bonbons after dinner. A midnight supper might include fried oysters, Welsh rabbit, deviled crabs, lobster, caviar with lemon juice, or scrambled eggs and bacon.

Three orchestras, usually violin, cello, piano and sometimes harp, would play all evening, except for interludes when a piano player was paid by music publishers to introduce and publicize such tunes as "After the Ball."

Before the Everleigh House opened, according to *Come Into My Parlor*, the Everleigh's definitive biography by Charles Washburn, the working girls were given evening gowns and daily drills in conduct. Minna said, "Be polite and forget what you are here for. Gentlemen are only gentlemen when properly introduced. We shall see that each girl is properly presented. No lining up. There shall be no cry 'in the parlor girls' when the visitors arrive. The Everleigh Club is not for the rough element, the clerk on a holiday or a man without a check book." (In fact, in later years, no one was admitted without a letter or card of introduction or a telephone recommendation from a previous patron, or unless he was known to the Club.)

Minna continued, "It means that your language will have to be lady-like . . . You have the whole night before you and one $50 client is more desirable than five $10 ones. Less wear and tear . . ."

The prices opening night were $10, $25 and $50, and they quickly escalated until no man spent less than $200 a night at the Everleigh House. Many men would spend as much as $1,000 in a single night during an era when a good worker might earn $6 a week. One competitor snorted, "I've heard of Southern hospitality, but not at these prices . . . " Champagne was $12 a bottle, dinner was $50, and that did not include a trip upstairs to the nearly soundproof boudoirs.

On opening night, champagne salesmen contributed their wares, as did those selling steaks and chickens. They figured it would be good advertising.

For more than a decade after that, the Everleigh Sisters would gross over $2,000 a night, sometimes reaching $5,000 a night, with personal profits of between $300 and $500 a day. They estimated that they banked $120,000 a year (with no taxes) during the club's existence.

They had succeeded beyond any whore's wildest dreams, and had in fact edged the house of prostitution into the realm of respectability.

They had rules:

"Contemplation of devilment was more satisfactory than the act itself."

"We do not like amateurs," so each Everleigh girl must have worked somewhere else before arriving in the Everleigh big leagues.

"To get in, a girl must have a pretty face and figure, must be in perfect health and must look well in evening clothes." Sounds like the qualifications for Miss America.

"Don't forget," Minna said, "entertaining most men at dinner or in any one of our parlors is more tiring than what the girls lose their social standing over."

Their girls were not a "commodity with a market-price like a pound of butter," Minna insisted. They were "much more on the same level with people belonging to professional classes who accept fees for services rendered."

The Everleigh Sisters also claimed, "If it weren't for married men, we couldn't have carried on at all and if it weren't for cheating married women we could have made another million."

The Everleigh Club was the starting point for innumerable stories.

Prince Henry, the brother of Kaiser William II, King of Prussia and the German emperor, visited the Club, where the ladies danced for him in fawn skins and tore a cloth bull to bits. Minna always enjoyed dances with mythological themes.

During dinner, a historic incident took place. One beautiful Everleigh girl began dancing the schottische on the table, but accidentally kicked off her slipper, which struck a glass of wine. A gallant gentleman immediately drank the wine from her slipper, after which each man removed a shoe of the woman sitting near him, filled it with champagne and toasted the Prince, the Kaiser and "beautiful women the world over." It was the first time champagne was drunk from a woman's slipper and it set a new standard for unhygienic gallantry the world over.

Lucy Page Gaston, the famous anti-cigarette crusader, was a regular visitor to the Club. She once shouted at Minna, "Your girls are going straight to hell!"

"What can I do?" asked Minna.

"Make them quit smoking cigarettes," was the response.

We know a great deal about the Everleigh Club because reporters were allowed in for free, as were state legislators. There are aging newsmen still alive in Chicago who remember the Everleigh Club, but none will admit ever going beyond the first floor.

There was even a scurrilous rumor that Marshall Field II was shot during a quarrel with a courtesan in the Everleigh Club. The family insisted he was accidentally shot at home, although newspapers sought to prove that his pistol could not have been fired without his premeditation—it had two safety catches. The rumor of Field's suicide attempt in the Everleigh Club still lurks about the city, aided by revelations that an Everleigh girl was offered $25,000 to say that she had seen Minna shoot him. Knowledgeable reporters of the time, after pursuing the story and the subsequent tale that it was suppressed because of the advertisements placed in their newspapers by Marshall Field & Co., concluded that it never happened. As one journalist commented, "If such a thing had occurred in the Everleigh bagnio, all the millions which the young man's father possessed could not have kept the boarders from blabbing."

The Everleigh Club was finally closed by the forces of reform and because the sisters began to advertise. It was one of the earliest instances of a media campaign gone awry.

The Everleighs were never shy or retiring women. They would proceed to make their daily bank deposits while driving in a carriage drawn by black horses and driven by liveried coachmen or, later, in a bright yellow open car. Each day they would be accompanied by their most beautiful courtesan, bejeweled, dressed in silk and satin, and waiting for them at the curb, a living commercial fattening tomorrow's deposit.

However, their trips to the bank did not directly lead to their downfall. What shocked the town was the 500 copies of a privately printed brochure, which the sisters hoped would make their establishment world famous. It said, with quiet dignity and charm, "While not an extremely imposing edifice without, it is a most sumptuous place within. 2131 Dearborn Street, Chicago, has long been famed for its luxurious furnishings, famous paintings, statuary and its elaborate and artistic decorations . . . Steam heat throughout, with electric fans in summer: One never feels the winter's chill or the summer's heat in this luxurious resort. Fortunate indeed, with all the comforts of life surrounding them, are the members of the Everleigh Club."

Perhaps the people of the time could accept brothels only if they were unheated in the winter and broiling in the summer. The town had often overlooked sin if a little suffering went along with it. But a heated, comfy whore house in winter was too much.

Mayor Carter Harrison II ordered the closing of the world's most famous brothel. The Everleighs approached the end of their business with dignity.

Minna told the Chicago American, "You get everything in a life time. Of course, if the Mayor says we must close, that settles it. What the Mayor says goes, as far as I am concerned. I'm not going to be sore about it, either. I never was a knocker, and nothing the police of this town can do will change my disposition. I'll close up shop and walk out with a smile on my face." Then she added, with a phrase which could either be a life's philosophy or the world's longest bumper sticker, "If the ship sinks, we're going down with a cheer and a good drink under our belts."

In a later statement, Minna estimated that the Levee was worth $15,000,000 in graft in the last few years, with her contribution being over $100,000. There were reports that if she had paid $20,000, a paltry sum, to a few influential aldermen, the Club might have remained open. She refused.

After 11 years in the business, the Everleigh Sisters had amassed almost $1,000,000 in cash; $200,000 in diamonds; $150,000 in books, paintings, tapestries, rugs, statues and furnishings, plus $25,000 owed—but never paid to them—by various clients. They also had 40 or 50 brass beds with specially built mattresses and those 20 gold-plated spittoons.

The final closing was delayed for 12 hours because of backstage maneuvering. Meanwhile, there was a party at the Club, with champagne for the hard-working journalists, toasts to the pianist, and tunes from the orchestras.

At 2:45 a.m., Oct. 25, 1911, there was a knock on the door. A big lieutenant said, "Sorry, girls, if it was us, you know how we'd be."

Minna asked, "What do we do now?"

The answer was straightforward, "Better clear out the house. Get rid of the guests."

Crowds were in front of the Club. Silk-hatted men, who didn't believe this was to be the final good-bye, lingered in the street.

But it was over. Within 24 hours, the famous courtesans of the Club had received hundreds of telegrams and telephone offers to work elsewhere.

When they left the business, Ada, the meek, quiet one, was only 35 years old and Minna was only 33. They took a six-month vacation in Europe and then tried to return to Chicago, but they were recognized. They couldn't work in the town which made them millionaires, so they spent the rest of their lives in New York, living off their earnings and proudly being members of a poetry reading circle of genteel ladies, who never suspected where the $15,000 gold-leaf piano in their apartment came from. They would tell the ladies that the piano, the statues and the furniture came from "an ancestor who was a gold miner and we inherited these priceless antiques" from him.

Minna died in 1948, Ada in 1960 at age 93.

Before she died, Minna asked, "We never hurt anybody, did we? We never robbed widows and we

made no false representations, did we? Any crimes they
attributed to us were the outcries of jealousy. We tried
to get along honestly. Our business was unholy, but
everybody accepted it. What of it?"

The Everleigh Sisters made a million dollars before
there were income taxes, kept most of it despite the
Depression, and lived comfortably all their lives.
There's either a moral or an immoral in that somewhere.

Chapter Two: Mayors

"I'm pretty old and fat, but I'll
guarantee to lick any Britisher
my weight."
    Big Bill Thompson, 1927

Chicago's pioneer mayors were good Yankees, serious, wealthy and often dull. Later, the city got political animals, wild men capable of causing beer riots or of firing the entire police force.

Some mayors were controlled by gamblers. Others led vast machines of workers who were beholden to them and their semi-secret mentors.

Every so often the electorate would suffer from a good-government spasm and good men would be elected. They would try to reform the town, closing down bars on Sundays, houses of prostitution on weekdays and raiding gambling dens within sight of City Hall. But the good that these men did was quickly interred with the end of their administrations, as the citizens, time after time, would vote for the loudest, most boastful rascal who promised an open town.

No mayor of Chicago has ever gone on to become President. Or senator. The job has been its own career cul-de-sac.

The best of the mayors have more or less let the town

rule them, enforcing the laws just enough so respectable citizens could walk the streets, but not causing enough trouble to scare off the tourists, conventioneers or local folks who wanted to drink, gamble or sin a little.

Chicago is a deeply religious town with a moral facade which thinly disguises a desire to wallow, more often than not, in sinful activities. It vacillates between loving sin for the money it brings and hating it for the morning after.

Its mayors have often epitomized this attitude, making deals with crooks and gangsters while issuing pious statements about how awful crime is.

If all the mayors of Chicago could sit down and tell their favorite stories, most would pick a good bar, with beer or cheap brandy. If they knew the public was observing them, the forum would take place at a church's pulpit and the stories would be about bridges built, streets widened and schools improved.

What follows are the stories the mayors might tell if they sat in a saloon, swilling legal and illegal hooch and patting their full paunches—I cannot find a single important, effective *thin* Mayor in Chicago's past history!

THE MAYOR WITH STYLE

William B. Ogden said, "I was born close to a sawmill, was cradled in a sugar trough, christened in a mill pond, early left an orphan, graduated from a log schoolhouse and, at 14, found I could do anything I turned my hand to and that nothing was impossible, and ever since, madame, I have been trying to prove it, with some success."

His life makes that statement a truth. Ogden, who was Chicago's first mayor, built the city's first railroad (the Galena & Union, now the Chicago & Northwestern), was the first president of the Union Pacific Railroad, built the first drawbridge across the Chicago River, helped create the Illinois-and-Michigan Canal, was first president of Rush Medical College, was a wealthy real estate speculator and bankrolled International Harvester when he gave Cyrus McCormick $25,000 so he could build a reaper-works in Chicago.

But he didn't start that way. When Ogden arrived in muddy, gooey Chicago, the village had just built its first public building—a pig pen. His relatives had bought $100,000 worth of Chicago real estate and Ogden was sent to look it over. After he saw that the land was ankle deep in muddy water, he wrote, "You have been guilty of the grossest folly."

He quickly changed his mind. That summer, when the land was dry, he sold a third of it for $100,000. That led him to believe that perhaps Chicago had a future. The belief was confirmed when he bought some land for $8,000, held it for a few years and sold it for $3,000,000.

Ogden was elected mayor on May 2, 1837. Even then, during the city's first mayoral contest, the Democratic Party was accused of "large-scale election fraud," according to journalist-historian Kenan Heise. Since there were only 4,170 people in town, and chances are everyone knew everyone else, the depth of the fraud is open to question.

While Ogden was mayor (1837-38), there was a banking panic in the country. Illinois would later go bankrupt. Folks demanded that Chicago not honor its debts. But Ogden shouted, "Do not tarnish the honor of our infant city." After he said that, Chicagoans agreed to pay off the city's debts somehow. Ogden's statement has been remembered by historians for generations, and has been honored for all time. I wonder. After Ogden said that, the city issued its own money, called scrip, so commerce could continue until taxes could be collected. I have never understood how a call for questionable currency could become the most heroic statement of the first Mayor of Chicago.

Later, Ogden and his friend, Walter L. Newberry, were instrumental in the building of Holy Name Cathedral, perhaps the city's most illustrious church. But the two men did not act out of piety. In keeping with Chicago's tradition that politics needn't compete with concern about one's place in heaven, the two men donated the block on which the church now stands in exchange for the Catholic vote for a new bridge over the Chicago River. The bridge was needed so land owned by Newberry and Ogden could be developed and sold. The bridge—and the church—were built, providing an example of politics saving souls.

It may be that Ogden will be remembered, not for saving Chicago's infant reputation, building its rail-roads, starting its brewing industry (he did that, too), or nearly single-handedly creating the city. He may be remembered for all time for his style.

Ogden once ordered a set of china for himself, to be imported from China. However, the ship carrying it was wrecked. Years later, while visiting the Mediterranean, his host served him on some very, very familiar-looking china. While the two men talked, the host revealed that the dishes were part of a shipwrecked cargo which the host had bought at bargain prices. Ogden finished his meal, but never revealed that he was eating off his own dinnerware. That's style!

THE ALMOST-TREASONOUS MAYOR

Only one Chicago ex-mayor was arrested for possible treason, although perhaps many deserved to be.

Buckner Smith Morris was the city's second Mayor (1838) and he did practically nothing memorable while holding that office.

During the Civil War, he was a member of the Sons of Liberty, a Southern-loving group. He was arrested on suspicion of disloyalty in 1864 during the great Camp Douglas escape scare. It was widely rumored that Southerners were going to free and arm the thousands of prisoners in Camp Douglas in Chicago in hopes that they would sack the city and create a second front during the war.

Morris was arrested mainly because his wife often supplied clothing to the prisoners. He was taken to Cincinnati (surely a worse fate than being shot or sent to the gallows), where he was tried by court-martial and acquitted. Later, his wife left him.

The "Know Nothings" Who Knew Nothing about Germans

The moral to this story is: Never, ever interfere with a Chicagoan's right to drink beer. It is, and always will be, an inalienable right. Hell, it's even important.

In the early 1850's, a wave of pro-American sentiment swept the country and created the Native American, or "Know Nothing," party. Its slogan was: "Put none but Americans on guard," meaning that only the native-born should be on the police force, in politics and in control of American life.

Dr. Levi Day Boone became the embodiment of that philosophy in Chicago and was elected mayor despite the fact that the town was half German and Irish.

Dr. Boone was the grand-nephew of bear-killer, Indian-fighter and explorer Daniel Boone. He received his education at something called the Transylvania Medical University in 1829. That should have told folks something about the doctor, but they elected him anyway.

In keeping with his political philosophy, Dr. Boone demanded that all applicants for city employment, especially those on the newly organized police force, be able to prove they were born on American soil. That angered a few folks, but it did not create a riot and near-insurrection.

Dr. Boone's other decisions did.

Chicago had a Sunday closing law which hadn't been enforced for a dozen years. Dr. Boone and his police applied that law in a most peculiar way. Only beer halls, which were mainly located on the North Side with its German population, would be shut. Saloons which sold whiskey, and which were on the South Side, were permitted to open their side and back doors for business.

Dr. Boone also recommended that the saloon licensing fee be increased by 600 per cent (!) from $50 to $300 a year.

Owners of hundreds of German beer halls refused either to close or to pay the higher licensing fee. More than 200 people were arrested, despite the fact that orators in the German community were shouting that they would rather die than submit to these outrages on their rights.

The beer hall owners' trial was scheduled for April 21, 1855. That morning a mob of more than 400 Germans, preceded by a fife and drum corps, marched on the Court House Square. Their representatives entered the courtroom and announced to Judge Henry C. Rucker that any guilty findings against any of the defendants would start a riot. One writer noted that they threatened Rucker by saying that "the decision of the court must be in their favor if the town didn't want war." But then Chicago has never been renowned for its peaceful trials.

The mob then left the courtroom and stopped all traffic at Randolph and Clark Streets, adjoining the court, until Luther Nichols, Captain of the Police, attacked. Cops armed with clubs charged into the mob, which broke and ran. Shots were fired and a newspaper story of the day reported that (soon-to-be) famed detective Allan Pinkerton was almost killed, "being shot by a policeman who had become crazy with the excitement of the scene." More excitement was to follow.

The mob retreated to the North Side and made plans. At 3 p.m., they returned, more than 1,000 strong and armed with shotguns, rifles, clubs, pistols, swords, butcher knives and hammers. They were getting serious.

But the mayor also had a strategy. Every cop in town was brought to the Public Square, plus 150 deputies, giving the Mayor a defense force of 250 men. Cannons were placed near City Hall.

As the rioters approached the Clark Street Bridge, the mayor ordered the tender to swing the draw, opening the bridge and preventing the mob from crossing. According to *History of the Chicago Police* (1887) by John J. Flinn, "A howl went up that was heard in the Court House Square. They (the mob) demanded that the bridge-tender close the draw at once. They threatened him with death. They coaxed him with honeyed words. They offered bribes. Some talked of shooting him."

The draw was finally swung back into place and the mob swarmed across to meet the 250 police and deputies formed into a line. There were shorts of "Pick out the stars" or "Shoot the police" and shoot they did. In fact, the action of the mob in 1855 makes the 1968 Democrat Convention riots look tame by comparison.

There was a pitched battle, a gun-and-knife fight in

the heart of town over the right to drink beer on Sundays!!

A German, Peter Martin, shot off Patrolman George W. Hunt's arm with a blast from a shotgun. Martin was then killed.

The fight continued for more than an hour. Both sides expended a lot of ammunition and the mob finally retreated, taking the wounded with them. To this day there are unconfirmed rumors that more than one man died in the battle (one is the official death statistic) and the casualties were secretly buried days later in quiet German funerals. The North Siders didn't want the police to know the extent of the German wounds.

Patrolman Hunt was arrested after German saloon owners complained, but he was released and was later voted a $3,000 reward by the City Council.

Of the 60 people arrested during the Lager Beer Riots, only 14 were tried and only two were found guilty of anything. Those two, Irishmen named Farrell and Halleman, were granted new trials, which were never held. Historian Herbert Asbury wrote that "it seemed little less than a travesty on justice that in a sedition notoriously German, the only victims should be two Irishmen." So the city forgot about its charges against Farrell and Halleman.

The Know Nothing Party quickly faded from view and Boone was never again elected mayor. During an election two months after the riot, voters soundly defeated a prohibition law.

And all the worry and turmoil proved only that no

one should interfere with a Chicagoan who wants to drink beer, something the nation forgot when Prohibition became law 64 years later.

ON KNOWING WHEN TO QUIT

Isaac L. Milliken worked his way up from shoeing horses and talking politics to mayor of Chicago in 1854. No other man in Chicago history can make that claim, and few would want to try.

Once he left the office of mayor, it was said that he never worked with horses again, a testimony to the political process.

A FABLE ULTIMATELY ABOUT THE WILLINGNESS TO SUPPORT CULTURE

John B. Rice was a political rarity in the days before Ronald Reagan—a professional actor who became a successful politician.

Rice, who was mayor from 1865 to 1869, a time when the city was booming in population, was also a famous theater owner of his day.

Unfortunately, his early desire to enrich the culture of the local folks ended in a quick disaster.

A troup from Milwaukee came to Chicago to present Vincenzo Bellini's "La Sonnambula" on July 30, 1850. It was to be Chicago's first opera.

The four people from Milwaukee were aided by local singers and musicians, and it looked as though Chicago was about to enter big time culture. After about an hour of singing, the audience heard people outside the theater warning that there was a fire.

But Rice rushed to the stage and yelled, according to historian A. T. Andreas, "Sit down! Sit down!! Do you think I would permit a fire to occur in my theater? Sit down!" The man must have been quite persuasive, because the audience returned to its seats until the smoke and flames made it quite obvious that a fire was burning the theater with or without Rice's permission. That ended Chicago's first opera season, which lasted just over one hour.

During the fire, one drunken opera enthusiast decided to remain in the theater. Identified only as "Mr. B.", he had been cheering every pause in the score with an enthusiastic "Bravo." Before his friends finally dragged him from the burning theater, he sat alone in the front row shouting at the mounting flames, "Bravo! Bravo! The most splendid imitation of a fire I ever saw!"

Later, to help Rice recoup his losses, the opera company gave him a benefit performance at City Hall. Andreas, with just a hint of sarcasm, wrote, "The profundity of the alleged sympathy (for Rice's theater, which burned to the ground) was manifested by the numbers—who remained away from the concert."

The benefit raised a grand total of $60 for Rice. Opera in Chicago was then as near-terminal as Carmen in her final act.

ALL THIS ON A QUART OF BRANDY A DAY

He fired the entire Chicago police force. He personally

caught and arrested gamblers. He lost a fist fight with a private detective. He introduced the Prince of Wales by practically slapping him on the back. He tore down advertising signs which offended him and he illegally leveled an entire neighborhood.

Long John Wentworth was certainly colorful. In fact, if he were any more colorful, Chicago might not have been standing after he finished his terms as mayor.

Long John arrived in Chicago barefoot at age 21 on Oct. 25, 1836 and was owner of a local newspaper by Nov. 23, only four weeks later. By age 28, he was in Congress, resisting the sweet nothings whispered in his ear by the representatives of Wisconsin. Wisconsin wanted to become a state and it needed Chicago's population to do that. The folks from Wisconsin offered Long John the following deal: Vote for redrawing the boundaries of Wisconsin at the southernmost tip of Lake Michigan so Chicago would become part of Wisconsin and we'll make you our first Senator. You can also hand pick Wisconsin's first governor.

But Long John didn't want to become a citizen of Wisconsin. As a result, Chicago remained part of Illinois so that its northern-leaning population would counterbalance the Southern-sympathizing part of the state. Illinois remained in the Union during the Civil War. If Long John had voted otherwise, Illinois might have seceded and the Civil War might have taken a very different turn.

Earlier, in 1818, Illinois had entered the Union the Chicago way—illegally. No more than 30,000 people were living here at the time, although 40,000 were needed

"Long John" Wentworth, 1847.

for statehood. United States marshalls counted everyone
in the state—including those just passing through on
covered wagons or on horseback. Sometimes different
marshalls would count the same family again and again
and again. (It was just the beginning of a long history of
crooked voting in this region.)

Wentworth returned to Chicago and became Mayor
on March 3, 1857, after a violent campaign during
which one man was killed and several others were
wounded near the polling places.

At the time, he was six feet six inches tall, weighed
about 300 pounds with feet 14 inches long and six inches
wide. His philosophy of life was, "Eat when you're
hungry, drink when you're thirsty, sleep when you're
sleepy and get up when you're ready."

He would usually order 30 to 40 courses for a single
dinner and would insist that everything be placed on the
table before him when he was ready to eat, from soup to
ice cream. Then, sitting alone at a table normally used
for five or more people, he would whirl the table around
until the dish he wanted was within reach. His daily
consumption of brandy was between a pint and a quart.
It seemed to provide enough fuel for him.

Early in his administration, Long John decided that
low hanging advertising signs would have to go. The
Mayor didn't want to bump his head on them any more.
On June 18, 1857, he gathered all the police and express
wagon drivers in the city, prepared them for their
mission by personally pouring shots of bourbon for
them, and ordered them to remove, "every swinging
sign, awning post or box found protruding two feet or

more beyond the front of the buildings." All these signs
were thrown into a pile on State St., where their owners
could retrieve them if they wished.

Emmett Dedmon wrote in *Fabulous Chicago* that one
sign was "a great pair of false teeth under a glass bell
that by means of compensating springs were made to
masticate the air for 25 days at a time." The dentist who
was the subject of that unique advertisement later
placed a notice in the local papers saying, "Long John or
one of his imps or someone else stole my sign away but
not my official instruments. I remain at 77 Lake Street,
Tremont Block."

Having once taken matters into his own hands, Wentworth did it again. In fact, creating the rules and laws as
he went along became a habit with him.

For instance, one hot summer afternoon, according to
historian Herbert Asbury, two police officials entered
the second floor window of Burrough's Place, notorious
gambling den. When the gamblers saw these doughty
minions of the law, they rushed out of the place through
the front door and directly into the waiting arms of the
Mayor, all 300 pounds of him. Wentworth then personally supervised the booking of the 18 prisoners and
announced that anyone with a city license who bailed
them out would lose his license. This was a real threat to
owners and taxi drivers (hackmen).

Later, Charlie Cameron, the gamblers' lawyer,
appeared at the jail and demanded to speak to his
clients. His request was denied. When he was seen
talking to a gambler through the bars of a window to
the jail, Wentworth personally grabbed the attorney

and locked him up. And when the gamblers finally got out of jail, they found that the police had taken everything from their establishment. Burrough's Place never re-opened.

These days, with so many lawyers richly deserving a night or two in jail for writing unintelligible laws or for being smartasses, it's a wonder that more mayors do not follow Wentworth's example.

Long John's next exploit did not involve merely a single gambling den. He expanded his horizons and decided to level an entire neighborhood illegally.

The Sands, a center of vice in Chicago, had been an eyesore for years. The inhabitants included Mike O'Brien, Jr., a pimp for his four sisters, and Dutch Frank, owner of a kennel of fighting dogs and of a bar with a bartender "whose nose and ears had been chewed off in fights," according to historian Herbert Asbury. It cost just 25 cents to be with the women in Freedy Webster's place, but it was 50 cents at Anna Wilson's house. Once Ms. Wilson lost one of her best girls because Mother Herrick, another whorehouse owner, offered the lady a clean dress. In retaliation, Gentle Annie (about whom you'll read more later), three other women and a bunch of pimps attacked Mother Herrick's establishment with clubs, beat Mother Herrick and her girls, and took the best of Herrick's ladies back to Anna Wilson. Visiting the Sands was nothing to write home to mother about.

Little could be done to clean up the Sands because the

ownership of the property was involved in a court battle. That is, nothing could be done until Long John decided to take action.

It was rumored that Long John Wentworth arranged the dog fight between Dutch Frank's champion and a dog owned by Bill Gallagher, a butcher. The winner would get $250 and every able-bodied man from the Sands went to the other side of town to watch the fight. Then the Mayor attacked.

On April 20, 1857, "in a moral spasm," according to A. T. Andreas, Long John Wentworth marched across the Clark Street Bridge leading more than 30 policemen and hundreds of citizens. Early that afternoon, nine houses were literally torn down by hooks and chains, while the mob stole everything it could. Around 4:30 p.m., the remaining houses in the Sands burned to the ground.

Newspapers once complained that "the most beastly sensuality and the darkest crimes have had their homes in the Sands." After the Mayor acted, the inhabitants of the Sands spread their vices throughout the city. Wentworth probably filed the experience under "the best-laid plans of mice and men, etc."

Undaunted, he proceeded to fire the entire police force of the city of Chicago!

Perhaps Wentworth was just doing too much, what with making his own arrests, writing laws, designing uniforms and badges, and everything else. Local folks didn't like his handling of the police force and they convinced the State Legislature to create a board of three police commissioners to take control of local police out of the Mayor's hands.

This upset Long John Wentworth, and people should have know better than to upset Long John.

On March 26, 1861, the Chicago Tribune carried the following story:

The Chicago police is no more. It ended its career abruptly.

At 20 minutes before 2 o'clock a.m., His Highness the Mayor assembled the entire force in his office in the Court House and [after calling them 'America's finest,' according to another source] discharged them in a body. The order for their assembling was issued exactly at midnight. The men were recalled from their beats as suddenly as possible. Some were brought . . . from the vicinity of the graveyard and its ghosts; and others from the neighborhood of Bridgeport and its brigands.

The astonished guardians of the night were told they were discharged and that their official duties had ended . . . The city was turned over to burglars, robbers and incendiaries. And from that hour to the present, Chicago has been without the protection of watch- men . . .

The offense (of firing the entire police force) deserves punishment in the penitentiary, but unfortunately it had not been provided against by the statute, for the reason that it was not deemed possible that such an act would ever be committed, on the same principle that the Spartans had no rule for the punishment of parricides (father killers) . . .

In the South, he (Wentworth) would have been tarred
and feathered . . . In Chicago, however, there is a different standard for the reward of extraordinary public
service. Here it will pass with many for a smart trick
and he elicited loud laughter from fools and pimps,
though decent citizens severely censure the wicked deed
and grieve that . . . the guilty offender will go un-
whipped by justice.

(The Tribune, in its righteous wrath, may have exag-
gerated. After all, Wentworth left custodians in the
police stations and told his men to be ready to return if
Long John rang the town bells.)

The time estimates vary as to how long Chicago was
without police protection. Some say it was as short as
12 hours, others say it was as long as 36 hours before the
police board, which had been slow to act before Wentworth's firings, began to rehire the constables.

There were ingrates who said that, except for a few
daylight robberies, the city hardly knew the difference.
The old police force was that inept.

The Prince of Wales, later to become King Edward
VII, was Chicago's first royal visitor. When he stopped
by in 1860, Long John and the Prince shared the same
balcony of the Prince's hotel. Long John introduced the
Prince to the assembled townsfolk this way: "Boys, this
is the Prince of Wales. He's come to see the city and I'm
going to show him around. Prince, there are the boys."
It would rank among Wentworth's most famous
statements.

When the Prince thanked Long John for an enjoyable
visit, Wentworth interrupted, "Never mind: We treat

everybody that way out West." And when Wentworth was asked how he felt sitting next to the future king of England, he corrected his questioner this way: "I was not sitting beside the Prince. He sat beside me."

Wentworth's ego knew no bounds. An author once submitted a new history of Chicago to Wentworth for his approval. Long John scratched out all entries which didn't refer to him and returned the manuscript, saying, "There, young man, is a correct history of the city!"

There were only two known instances of Long John backing down on anything.

A big Irishman was promised a job on the police force in exchange for swaying some votes in Long John's favor. After Long John's election the Irishman showed up, but Wentworth said, "We think you fellows are very nice before you vote, but when we get your ballot you can go to hell." Long John was never known for his diplomacy.

Wentworth's statement visibly upset the Irishman, who demanded to "step outside" with the Mayor. Wentworth gave him a job on the police force.

On another occasion, after Wentworth had been drinking, he got into an argument with Allan Pinkerton, who had organized a private guard agency. Wentworth outweighed his opponent (and any other two men in town), but Pinkerton was in better condition. The fight was settled after Pinkerton hit Wentworth in the belly and kicked him into the gutter.

Before he died, Wentworth bought a huge burial plot so that "if I get tired of lying on my back, I will have room to turn over and kick."

He died on Oct. 16, 1888, and was buried beneath a 65-foot tall tombstone of his own design. It had no inscription on it. Earlier, when asked about that peculiarity, Wentworth said, "If there is no inscription on my monument, people will ask: 'whose monument is that?' On being informed that it is John Wentworth's monument, they will ransack the libraries to find out who John Wentworth was. When they have found out, they will remember."

Few people remember Long John today and fewer still ransack libraries searching out his stories. That's too bad. He was an American original.

REMEDY THINGS IN SOME WAY, I THINK

Every once in a while the voters of Chicago would rise up and throw the bums out. That happened in 1869, when Roswell B. Mason was elected mayor on the People's Party ticket because, as one historian noted, "the peculations and defalcations of office holders were matters of public notoriety." (Imagine everyone in town knowing about an office holder's "defalcations.")

Anyway, Mason, an engineer, worked hard, but his work was interrupted by the Great Fire of 1871, after which he asked that all citizens exercise great caution in the use of fire, thus firmly closing the barn door after the horse was fried. He also closed saloons at 9 p.m. for a week after the fire and recommended a day of "prayer and humiliation." By all accounts, he did a good job after the fire, but he never quite ended corruption in Chicago. But then no one else did either.

He should be remembered because he was the first mayor to say that the number of saloons should be limited. This demand was in his annual message of 1870. Mason pointed out that there was one saloon for every 130 inhabitants of the city. If only men over age 21 were counted, there was one saloon for every 26 men. He said, "That this state of things should be remedied in some way, I think, does not admit of doubt . . . " If you think about what he said, that statement becomes slightly, well, forgettable.

HARRISON, PERE ET FILS

Chicago had two mayors named Carter Harrison, father and son, and between them they held office for over two decades.

The elder Harrison was first elected in 1879 and was last elected in 1893, in time to be the mayor during the Columbian Exposition. It was suspected at the time that Harrison got the mayor's job both because he looked more like a theatrical version of a distinguished mayor than anyone else in town and because he would let gambling and prostitution run unmolested.

For instance, he made a deal with Mike McDonald, a leader and long-time representative of the criminal classes of Chicago. The two men agreed that no one's pocket would be picked at the entrance to the fair. After all, the businessmen with concessions inside the fair wanted the folks at least to enter the fair before their money departed.

According to Finis Farr's *Chicago*, the agreement

specified that any pickpocket arrested at the gates to the
fair would have to return the loot either to the victim or
to the arresting officer and would have to pay the
copper $10. In exchange, it was agreed that any pick-
pocket arrested in the city's central area during daylight
hours would be released immediately from the Central
Station House. In other words, pickpockets were given
the middle of the city as their territory.

(By the way, it was during the jockeying for which
city would get the Columbian Exposition that Chicago
won the title "Windy City." Chicago, New York,
Washington and St. Louis were all vying for the honor
of being host for the fair, but Chicago was boasting
more than the other towns. This led Charles A. Dana,
writing in the New York Sun, to advise his readers to
ignore "the nonsensical claims of that windy city." It
was the first use of the term, and it had nothing to do
with gusts felt at State and Madison.)

The 183 days of the Fair were, by all accounts, a re-
sounding success. Whorehouse rents tripled, but the
ladies made money. Gentleman Jim Corbett, Diamond
Jim Brady, John Phillip Sousa and Lillian Russell visited
Chicago during the fair, as did a hygienically stuffed
whale, which was docked at Clark St. so the rubes could
walk through it.

Princess Eulalia of Spain provided controversy during
the fair when she snubbed Mrs. Potter Palmer, the local
society queen, by refusing to meet with the wife of an
innkeeper (Potter Palmer created State St. as a shopping
center of the city and was much more than a mere innkeeper). Mrs. Palmer got her revenge years later when

Mrs. Potter Palmer c. 1905.

CHICAGO HISTORICAL SOCIETY

she was invited to meet the Princess, and Mrs. Palmer said, "I cannot meet this bibulous representative of a degenerate monarchy." So there!

The World's Columbian Exposition was supposed to celebrate the 400th anniversary of Columbus' discovery of America, in 1492. But because of one thing and another, the 1492 landing was celebrated a year late and few people complained about that. The Fair was an astounding success and it attracted 25,836,073 visitors. That meant that nearly half the population of America at the time saw the Exposition!

The sensation of the Fair was Fahreda Mahzar, who as Little Egypt wore diamonds on her garters, a heavy skirt and a thick brassiere. Nevertheless, she wowed the rubes, easily beat Peerless Annabelle, the serpentine dancer (you could see every muscle in her body) for the title of sexiest dancer at the fair. Little Egypt later became Mrs. Andrew Spyropoulis, wife of a Chicago restaurant owner. One old timer commented, "Today women wear less to go to the grocery store than Little Egypt wore in 1893."

Folks tended to get quite eloquent about the Fair. Read this:

We are now in Machinery Hall. Just think of it!
Seventeen acres of palpitating iron and steel lie before
us! . . . One does not need to be a mechanic to be interested in the machinery before us. Each part is
performing some wonderful task, as though possessed
of intelligence. Man seems a weak being beside these
forceful servants of his, which obey his slightest touch

. . . Great steam-hammers are at work nearby and
mighty derricks and cranes seem engaged in friendly
rivalry. Great is the domain of the human mind.

Once a visitor left the Fair, the joys of Chicago
awaited him. Within a block of City Hall, there stood a
wide-open gambling den, complete with roulette and
stud poker tables. In fact, demands for roulette wheels
for Chicago were so great that the ordinary source of
supply in New York couldn't handle all the orders. A
Chicago factory had to be started.

In the typical flowery language of the day, William T.
Stead described the deal between Harrison, a descen-
dant of Princess Pocahontas and a Virginia landowner,
and the gamblers. Stead wrote in *If Christ Came to
Chicago:*

"Before Carter Harrison's last election, a certain
number of gamblers, as is the custom in this city, made
up a purse and subscribed several thousands of dollars
to Mr. Harrison's election fund. When he was elected,
he took steps to recoup those patriots who had supplied
him with the sinews of war." Under Mike McDonald's
direction, a gambling syndicate was formed, with 40 to
65 per cent of the profits from all illegal establishments
going to the syndicate in return for freedom from police
interference. Eventually, some of that gambling money,
which amounted to a "colossal fortune" (Stead) during
the World's Fair, reached Harrison. Chicago was then
"the most wide-open town that America had ever seen,
or probably ever will see," according to one historian.

Harrison's demise came suddenly. He was sitting in

his easy chair at home during the waning days of the Fair. Because the Mayor had no guards of any sort, Patrick Eugene Joseph Prendergast walked into his home. Before that, Prendergast had visited Adolph Kraus, the Corporation Counsel for the city. Kraus, according to writer Harry Barnard, had received several threatening postcards from Prendergast, who wrote in red ink "I want your job." "Do not be a fool. Resign," and "Third and final notice. You either resign or I will remove you."

When Prendergast arrived, Kraus, no fool, humored him by telling him the job was his. Prendergast got flustered and said he didn't want the job that day and left.

Prendergast was a religious nut and a political fanatic (an explosive combination) who thought it was his divine duty to force the elevation of street car tracks in the city. He expressed his anger by firing five shots into Harrison, killing him instantly.

Harrison's funeral featured his riderless horse following his hearse. No one ever rode that mare again.

By most accounts, Carter Harrison II, the first Chicago-born Mayor, ran a much tighter ship than his father did. He helped crush Charles T. Yerkes, the traction baron, and he once refused a $500,000 bribe. For that alone he should be honored in Chicago history.

During his first campaign for Mayor in 1897, he was pictured with both hands in his pockets, leading local folks to say they were thankful at last Chicago might get a Mayor who finally keeps his hands in his *own* pockets.

When he entered office, he described the City Council as:

a motley crew . . . Saloonkeepers, proprietors of gambling houses, undertakers . . . A rare conglomeration of city fathers ruled Chicago in the '90s, (a city) whose citizens for years, from lack of interest, supineness, or from absolute stupidity, had permitted the control of public affairs to be the exclusive appendage of a low-browed, dull witted base-indeed gang of pug-uglies, with no outstanding characteristic beyond an unquenchable lust for money . . . .

Those words could describe many Chicago City Councils down through history.

The men starring in the City Council of the late 1890s included "Hot Stove" Jimmy Quinn, who claimed his buddies would steal anything they could get their hands on, even a hot stove; Johnny Powers, who bought votes in the City Council for about $10 apiece; "Umbrella Mike" Boyle, who collected his bribes in an umbrella; and Mike McInerney, who once said that smoke from the stockyards was good for babies.

Things got so bad in town that Harrison once suggested that the good citizens "might carry revolvers strapped outside their clothing" for protection.

However, by the last year of Harrison's final administration (1911-1915) Chicago was as free of vice as it ever had been. In fact, Harrison II was able to say during his final message on April 3, 1915:

There has been no official corruption in these 12 years, nor have friends grown rich at the expense of the public. Indeed, there have been practically no scandals in the City Hall. Heads of departments have been appointed for their honesty and efficiency; when they failed in measuring up to the right standard they have been relieved from duty. Contracts have invariably been let to the lowest bidder, contractors have been compelled to do good work . . . .

That state of affairs would not last for long.

THE MAYOR WAS A BAR BRAWLER

There was no indication that Fred A. Busse would reform anything. After all, he was a bar brawler, a friend of two-gun gangsters and a supporter of boozing on Sunday. Indeed, during his term he personally suspended the lawful closing time for his favorite saloon and he raided the Illinois Athletic Club after he was insulted during a card game there.

His gangster friend was Christian "Barney" Bertsche, who killed a detective and two cops shortly after Busse took office in 1907.

Busse's raid on the Illinois Athletic Club resulted in the Mayor losing a friend. Big Bill Thompson, who was given a key to the City Hall after Busse was elected, returned it after the raid, saying, "Fred Busse is unfit to be Mayor of this city." Busse replied, "Ha! Bill knew that key wouldn't unlock anything. That was to the temporary City Hall. I gave it to him when I knew we'd be moving to our new building."

During his administration, Busse ended the First Ward Ball, a regularly scheduled orgy (see Bathhouse

John Coughlin's story); helped create the Chicago Plan Commission, which eventually saved the lake front for the people; and reluctantly supported the 1911 Vice Commission report.

Busse, the crude, overweight, brawling ice-and-coal merchant, made no speeches during his election drive because he was injured in a train wreck. Anyway, he hated speeches. His term was marked with verbal explosions from his executive office as Busse would shout, "Get the big thieves! I'll back every honest copper." When accused of being too close to business interests, Busse merely said, "Go to hell." He was a man of few words.

When he died, the Chicago Journal newspaper noted, "Fred's widow was left with 15 cents. Fred never gave a bootblack less than a half dollar nor a cabdriver less than a bill for a tip."

But Chicagoans, being nosy folks, also learned after his death that he had a safe-deposit box filled with a huge block of stock indicating ownership in a company which sold all the manhole covers to the city. He was a reform mayor, but he didn't forget his old habits.

THE CARCASS OF A RHINOCEROS AND THE BRAINS OF A BABOON

When William Hale "Big Bill" Thompson began his political career, one of his sponsors said, "the worst you can say about him is that he's stupid."

When he was finally defeated, after three terms as Mayor spanning the worst days of Prohibition and

"Big Bill" Thompson crowning the Queen of the Stockyards, 1921.

gangster-rule in Chicago, his arch-enemy, the Chicago Tribune, wrote:

For Chicago, Thompson has meant filth, corruption, obscenity, idiocy and bankruptcy. He has given the city an international reputation for moronic buffoonery, barbaric crime, triumphant hoodlumism, unchecked graft and dejected citizenship. He nearly ruined the property and completely destroyed the pride of the city. He made Chicago a byword of the collapse of American civilization. In his attempts to continue this, he excelled himself as a liar and defamer of character . . .

But then the Chicago Tribune never subscribed to the adage that if you can't say something good about someone, don't say anything at all.

Thompson's early life was spent avoiding education. He headed West to become a cowboy, but he returned to Chicago after his father died. Eventually he achieved some local fame as captain of the Chicago Athletic Club's water-polo team, which was his only qualification for office when he ran the first time.

Voters in other parts of the country might question how and why experience as a water polo player and football captain of a private club's teams might qualify a man to become mayor. But other men with even fewer qualifications have risen to the top in Chicago politics.

Thompson first ran for alderman in 1900 after making a $50 bet in a poker game with friends who said he was afraid to run. His speeches were dull, his delivery listless and his face a deadpan. When it was time for him to smile or laugh, an associate would let a brick fall to the floor as a signal to Big Bill.

Thompson began in politics as a dumb but clean-living man, a champion athlete on the side of goodness and truth. During his first mayoral campaign, he shouted, "I tell you I am going to clean up Chicago." By his third campaign, Al Capone's office was decorated with portraits of three men—Washington, Lincoln and Thompson. It was rumored that Capone gave Thompson between $150,000 and $260,000 during that campaign.

His pro-German stands before World War I helped him win the 1915 election. In fact, he was often nick-named "Kaiser Bill."

A few years later, a huge controversy centered around his refusal to invite Marshall Joffre, hero of the Marne, and Rene Viviani, French minister of Justice, to Chicago as part of their nation-wide tour drumming up American support for their side in World War I. Thompson noted that Chicago was "the sixth largest German city in the world" and added that he didn't think all of the people of Chicago wanted the French-men there.

Joffre and Viviani were finally invited by the Mayor, but not before Teddy Roosevelt said, "We'll hang old Thompson to a sour apple tree."

After the visit, Thompson continued to oppose the "federal government's war." A bishop from Texas said, "I think that Mayor Thompson is guilty of treason and ought to be shot . . . What this country needs is a few first-class hangings. Then we could go on with our work of mobilization without fear of being stabbed in the back." Texans usually knew the proper solution for most political arguments.

During Thompson's terms, he carried a sawed off shotgun in his car. A local court once ordered Thompson and his associates to pay $2,245,604 to the city, the amount they allegedly plundered. Big Bill Thompson almost had a drunken nervous breakdown over that decision until it was thrown out on appeal.

He employed a henchman of Capone as city sealer, the person in charge of honest weights and measures.

After his first two terms as Mayor, there were so many scandals, indictments of friends and signs of obvious corruption that Thompson couldn't run again. Instead, he left town looking for headlines. He found them by organizing an expedition to the South Seas in search of a legendary "tree climbing fish." He told reporters, "I have strong reason to believe that there are fish that come out of the water, can live on land, will jump three feet to catch a grasshopper and will actually climb trees."

Thompson set sail on a ship named the Big Bill, with a crew which included one theater-owner who wore nothing but a jock strap most of the day. The expedition ended before the Big Bill ever left the Mississippi River.

Thompson was elected mayor in 1915, 1919 and 1927, but it was his final campaign and term which marked Big Bill as the wildest, most irresponsible, dangerous and corrupt Mayor in Chicago's history.

(That was a title with many contenders, but read on. You'll see that Big Bill won it going away.)

His 1927 campaign was incredibly vitriolic, and it was only exceeded by Big Bill's losing 1931 primary effort.

By 1927, Big Bill had lost his mentor, Fred Lundin, who ran his campaigns and bossed his patronage throughout most of his career. It was Lundin who, in commenting upon the great profits available to a winning politician in Chicago, exulted, "We're at the feedbox now. And we're going to keep eating."

Because he was no longer friendly with Fred "Poor Swede" Lundin and Dr. John Dill Robertson, another long-time supporter of Thompson's, Big Bill appeared on the stage of a Loop theater with two caged live rats. He called one "Doc" and explained, "I can tell him because he hadn't had a bath for 20 years until we washed him yesterday. But we did wash him and he doesn't smell like a billy goat any longer." He called the other rat "Fred" and asked it, "Wasn't I the best friend you ever had?"

Thompson also said, on another occasion, "The doc is slinging mud. I'm not descending to personalities." Then, without sensing any apparent contradiction, Thompson continued, "But let me tell you that if you want to see a nasty sight, watch Doc Robertson eating in a restaurant. Eggs in his whiskers, soup on his vest. You'd think he got his education driving a garbage wagon."

Back in 1927, Thompson's opponents could sling mud as well as the master could. Edward R. Litsinger, who opposed Thompson in the 1927 Republican primary, said, "Bill Thompson has the carcass of a rhinoceros and the brains of a baboon." Litsinger was driven to that comment after Thompson said, "Ed Litsinger lived back of the gashouse, and when he moved to the North Side he left his old mother behind." Few politicians' mothers have been verbally attacked, even during wide-open Chicago primaries.

During that same 1927 campaign, he spent a lot of time opposing the King of England, who certainly did not aspire to become Mayor of Chicago. Thompson even threatened to punch the King of England in the snoot if he ever entered the city.

He said, "I'm pretty old and fat, but I'll guarantee to lick any Britisher my weight." He added, "I wanta make the King of England keep his snoot out of America." He even attacked William McAndrew, the able school superintendent, because McAndrew was Scottish and that might mean he was a serf for the King. He called McAndrew the King's "lackey" and he managed to get McAndrew drummed out of office shortly after he was elected.

Although local newspapers said Thompson's campaign against the King of England was the "quintessence of piffle," he spent a lot of time after he was elected trying to get allegedly pro-British history books banned from the Chicago Public Library. A henchman of Big Bill's, Urbine J. "Sport" Herrmann, threatened to burn all the offending books on the lake front until a court injunction stopped him. It wouldn't have made much of a bonfire because the Thompsonite only found four offending volumes, one of which was dedicated to George Washington.

Thompson's election-night victory celebration aboard his Fish Fan Club ship in 1927 ended sadly. After drinking large quantities of Prohibition hooch, the 1,500 loyal followers overloaded the boat and stomped so heavily that the ship quivered and sank in six feet of water.

It was after that 1927 election that Will Rogers said, "They was trying to beat Bill with the better element vote. The trouble with Chicago is that there ain't much better element."

Big Bill's Fish Fans Club, Belmont Harbor, 1925.

It was Thompson's advice to budding politicians, "If your opponent calls you a liar, call him a thief." He followed his own advice to the letter.

During the 1931 Republican Mayoral primary, when Thompson tried unsuccessfully to stay in office, he called his opponent, Municipal Judge John H. Lyle, "the nutty judge." The Chicago Daily News compiled most of the names each called the other, including:

William Halitosis Thompson
Blustering loudmouth, irresponsible mountebank
Jumbo the Flood Relief Quack
Moron
Blubbering jungle hippopotamus
Arrogant, incompetent, inefficient judge
Lazy blood-sucking jobbers
Lurching shambling imbecile
Flabby jowls of a barnyard hog
Blubbering charlatan
Sluggish being
Two jackass ears, a cowboy hat and an empty space in between
Chambermaid in a ranch bunkhouse

The newspaper asked, "Can both be right?"

As it turned out, both lost—Lyle to Thompson, Thompson to Cermak, the Democratic candidate.

Thompson's terms were marked by gangsterism throughout the city, especially at election time. During the Pineapple Primary in 1928, when hand grenades or "pineapples" were regularly used to convince the voters which way to cast their ballots, one Senator suggested that the Marines withdraw from Nicaragua and be sent to Chicago. That primary included the killing of "Diamond Joe" Esposito, who had been told "Get out of the ward; it's healthier for you"; the bombing of Judge John A. Swanson, who survived; the casting of 16 ballots from a horse stable which housed 16 horses but no humans; and the suggestion that all candidates sleep in hiding the night before the election.

It was a time when the bailiff of a Chicago court would closet himself with a defendant and negotiate the bribe for the judge. If the bailiff slapped the wall before re-entering the courtroom, the judge would know the defendant came up with the right price and the verdict would be assured.

When Big Bill Thompson died, on March 19, 1944, it was at first thought that he left an estate of only $150,000. That would indicate that all his energetic, self-congratulating shouts that he was honest, while the newspapers were crooked, were essentially correct. But, according to Wendt's and Kogan's definitive biography, *Big Bill of Chicago*, the money literally tumbled out when his safe deposit boxes were opened. One such box held $1,466,250 in cash, plus stocks, bonds and gold certificates. Another had $112,000 in stocks and bonds. Two more safe deposit boxes had $220,000 in stocks and $22,000 in $50, $100 and $500 bills. His estate totalled $2,103,024, most of it in cash and stocks secreted away in safe deposit boxes. No one knew how the money got there, although there were whispers, many, many whispers.

After his death, there was a battle between his

mistress of a dozen years, Ethabelle Green, who settled
for $250,000, and his wife, Maysie, who got most of the
estate. By the time she settled her lawyers' bills,
Ethabelle was left with only $100,000, not much for
giving the best years of her life to Big Bill.

The Daily News concluded that Big Bill Thompson
"was not a great man; he was a highly successful man in
his field. He was not a statesman, he was a consummate
politician. His success was based on deception and dis-
traction. He was the most amazingly unbelievable man
in Chicago's history."

Few disagreed.

"I'M GLAD IT WAS ME INSTEAD . . . "

On Feb. 15, 1932, Anton J. Cermak was shot in Bay-
front Park in Miami. Cermak was on the reviewing
stand and, after President-elect Franklin Roosevelt
made a short speech in an open car, he beckoned
Cermak to join him.

As Roosevelt's car was about to start, shots were
heard and Cermak, who was the Mayor of Chicago,
and four others were hit. They were shot by Guiseppe
Zangara, who later said he wanted to "kill all Presidents
. . . I have always hated the rich and the powerful."

There is general agreement about those facts. But
there is also a lot of mystery.

For instance, in December, 1932, Frank "The
Enforcer" Nitti was shot by a member of Cermak's
personal police detail. The detective was wounded in
the finger, while Nitti was shot three times. Some police

said Nitti was unarmed at the time of the killing. Others testified to Cermak's deadly fear of assassination. The detective who fired the shots said that Cermak "planned to stop all gangster operations during the (1933) World's Fair." The detective even threatened, it was said, to "blow the lid off Chicago politics." He was found guilty of assault, but was given a new trial which was never held.

All of that led to the rumors, never proven or adequately disproven, that Cermak died at Capone's orders. Nitti was a Capone henchman.

There were more mysteries. At the moment of the shooting, Cermak is supposed to have shouted, "The President, get him away!" and later he was supposed to have said to the President, "I am glad it was me instead of you." That last phrase was the most famous ever spoken by Mayor Anton Cermak.

However, there are those who say it ain't so. A reporter who was there told Ed Gilbreth, former political columnist for the Chicago Daily News, that "I am glad it was me instead of you" was created so the Chicago Herald American could have a good headline. That man insisted to the day he died that the reporter, not Cermak, made up those words. Cermak couldn't be taken to the hospital without saying anything. It just wouldn't make a good story.

Furthermore, Cermak didn't die of the bullets fired by Zangara. Cermak died of "ulcerative colitis," according to a doctor and a close friend of Cermak's. A report stated that the gunshot wounds had been completely cleaned and healed before Cermak's death. Dr. Karl

Meyer was quoted as saying, "The Mayor's life could have been saved if even a few days before he died the colitis could have been stopped."

This fact later led to a "psychosomatic analysis" of Cermak which stated that "the colitis patient . . . over-compensates for his passive, dependent wishes by re-verting to infantile expressions of achievement; that is with attacks of diarrhea . . . "

Not a very pleasant picture of a dynamic mayor.

Cermak, Chicago's first foreign-born mayor, was born in Prague, worked in coal mines in Illinois, started a real estate firm and for many years was the spokesman for the United Societies, a group ardently in favor of booze and against all prohibition.

He defeated Big Bill Thompson for Mayor in 1931, despite a typical Thompson campaign during which Big Bill said, "I won't take a back seat from that bohunk—Chairmock, Chermack or whatever his name is . . . Calls himself a 'Master Executive' . . . you Negroes know what a master is . . . who kicked all the Negro caddies off the golf courses? . . . Tony, the Jew-hater, supported by Rosenwald, the faker-philan-thropist . . . Tony, the German-hater . . . " and so on.

Cermak's achievements, after he took control of both the Democratic party and the Mayor's office, included nominating and electing Henry Horner, Illinois' first (and only) Jewish governor, and cutting into Irish control of Chicago politics. Of the 12 men nominated for judges in 1926, eight were Irish. In 1930, when Cermak handled the slating, of 14 Democratic nomi-nations for Municipal Court judge, only five were Irish.

With Cermak's death, a stop was put to that. A person of Irish descent occupied the Mayor's office in Chicago for the next four decades.

Cermak organized the Wet Vote and, for better or for worse, helped defeat Prohibition. He helped create the Democratic party of Chicago, something he isn't usually given credit for, by bringing together various ethnic groups and making sure they got a piece of the action. He didn't inconvenience local gangsters, but then few Chicago Mayors before or after Cermak have done much about that problem. He sought power, got it through infinite knowledge of the city's political organization, and then lost it because of a madman in Miami.

Chapter Three: Politicians Who Were Never Mayor

"Let the orgy be perfectly proper . . . "
Bathhouse John Coughlin, 1908

A Chicago politician was once asked if there was ever a good, honest, hard-working, brilliant alderman in the City Council. He said, "Sure there was—Paul Douglas, when he was the Fifth Ward alderman. But we kicked him upstairs to a lesser job and made him a U.S. Senator."

The person who heard that statement was dumbfounded. A U.S. Senator? That was being "kicked upstairs"? That was less powerful than being a Chicago alderman?

"Sure," said the local politician. "How many jobs does a Senator control compared to an alderman?"

He who controls the jobs has the loyalty of the troops and the votes on election day. The world—to say nothing of lucrative city contracts, insurance business, etc.—can be his. Down through history, the actual controllers of the jobs have often not been the mayor, who can be the city weakling. The town was then run either by the mayor's semi-secret mentor or by a strong city council.

The secret of the following tales is that you do not have to be mayor to be the subject of good stories. Often it's enough to be just a little crooked or quirky, with enough power to make it worth while for someone else to remember what you did or said.

Rotten Apples or Rotten Eggs?

Stephen A. Douglas, Senator from Illinois and debater of Abraham Lincoln, spent much of his career being in step with the Irish voters and out of sync with almost everyone else.

Douglas was a great compromiser who held few firm convictions about slavery (but then so did Lincoln). The great Lincoln-Douglas debates, historians often agree, were generally won by Douglas, although Lincoln went on to immortality, while Douglas faded into relative obscurity.

Douglas' worst moment in Chicago came on Sept. 1, 1854, when he was supposed to speak at North Market Hall in defense of his vote in favor of the Kansas-Nebraska Bill, which allowed new states to decide whether or not they would permit slavery within their borders. Many right-thinking people thought this was an unnecessary compromise which would allow the spread of slavery.

Douglas later said that his way from Washington to Chicago that year was lit by his burning effigies.

A mob of over 10,000 crowded around the Hall. They were determined to shout him down. One newspaper later noted that from "numerous orthodox Protestant

pulpits, especially of the Methodist and Baptist per-
suasion, the fiat went forth to the faithful that this anti-
Christ must be denied every opportunity to pollute the
pure atmosphere of Illinois with his perfidious breath."
The mob was ready to stop Douglas.

Douglas was undaunted. Historian Finis Farr, who
thought that Douglas' career was often marked by "a
firm touch on the wrong note," wrote that he spoke so
loudly he "could move leaves on a tree 300 feet distant
when he mounted the stump." He had the voice to challenge the mob, and he had the energy because, as Farr
also revealed, Douglas "often fueled in a barroom
before delivering an address."

Douglas surely needed fuel and any other help he
could get on that night in 1854. He battled that mob for
four solid hours. The crowd was "armed to the teeth in
anticipation of bloody violence," the Tribune noted.

One man, Douglas, stood before them, attempting to
exercise his freedom of speech. The Chicago Times
wrote that "Every name that vile tongues could invent
was hurled at him. In a moment, he was surrounded by
a howling, raging mob, hungry to do him personal
injury. But all undaunted, he fearlessly faced the enemy
. . . in defiance of yells, groans, catcalls and every in-
sulting menace and threat . . ."

Afterwards local historians disagreed about one vital
point. Some said he was pelted with rotten eggs while
facing the roaring mob. Others claimed he was hit with
rotten apples. The Times writer hoped to settle the
matter this way: "Perhaps as between rotten eggs and
rotten apples, there is not much choice of flavor, but the

Sunday Times historian . . . falls in line on the rotten apple side of this controversy." History rested easier after that statement.

After facing the howling, raging, rotten apple throwing mob for over four hours, after showing great personal bravery, Douglas heard the mob chant, "We won't go home until morning."

Douglas' classic reply, after being told that it was then past midnight, was "It is now Sunday morning— I'LL GO TO CHURCH AND YOU MAY GO TO HELL!"

BIG NOISE IN THE WIGWAM

Probably the biggest noise in Chicago history was heard on May 18, 1860, when Abraham Lincoln was nominated for the Presidency in Chicago in a two-story wooden hall called the Wigwam.

It was a carefully engineered moment, Chicago to its very core. Despite the candidate's insistence that no deals be made, a cabinet position was offered in exchange for Indiana's vote, and other jobs were promised to Ohio and Pennsylvania in exchange for Lincoln votes.

But hawk-nosed, cigar smoking, dignified W. H. Seward of New York was clearly in the lead for the nomination. He had the money, the power and the muscle of the New York delegation. He even had bands, uniforms and champagne, but he didn't have Chicago.

Behind the scenes, Lincoln supporters worked long, hard and dirtily to make sure their man would be nominated. They arranged for free transportation into the city for any and all Lincoln supporters. Pennsylvania, which was doubtful as to which way it would vote, was placed far away from Seward's New York delegation in the Wigwam seating arrangements.

When the day of the crucial vote arrived, the convention hall was jammed to the doors, meaning that Seward's men, who marched in their spiffy uniforms to the hall, weren't able to get inside.

During the first two ballots, Seward was ahead, but his lead was dwindling. Then came the moment the Lincoln men were waiting for. It was the third ballot. Lincoln had 231½ votes, just short of the 233 needed for the nomination.

David Kellog Cartter, a delegate from Ohio, stood and was recognized. A Cincinnati reporter, Murat Halstead, described Cartter as a "large man with rather striking features, a shock of bristling black hair, large and shining eyes and . . . terribly marked with smallpox. He has also an impediment in his speech which amounts to a stutter . . . "

So the jam-packed Wigwam delegates and the nation held its breath while this pock-marked, stuttering man, who was chairman of the Ohio delegation, began to speak. He slowly and agonizingly announced the "change of four votes of Ohio" to Mr. Lincoln.

"There was a moment's silence," Halstead wrote, and then "there was the noise in the Wigwam like the rush of a great wind in the van of a storm—and in another breath, the storm was there. There were thousands cheering with the energy of insanity." Some feared that the very walls of the Wigwam itself, built at a cost of $7,000, might tremble and fall because of the noise.

Then a man on the roof of the Wigwam yelled, "Fire the salute! Abe Lincoln is nominated!"

The cannon atop the Wigwam fired, the delegates inside the hall were dancing in the aisles, and the chairman banged his gavel so many times that the head broke off and struck a delegate, knocking him out. (Historian Finis Farr thought this incident led directly to the joke about the victim who comes to and mumbles, "Hit me again, I can still hear him.")

Men wept like children. When the cannon was fired, Halstead wrote,

The thunder of the salute rose above the din, and the shouting was repeated with such tremendous fury that some discharges of cannon were absolutely not heard by those on the stage . . . The city was wild with delight. The Old Abe men formed processions and bore rails through the streets. Torrents of liquor were poured down the hoarse throats of the multitude. A hundred guns were fired from the top of the Tremont House (Hotel) . . .

Only a few of the delirious Old Abe supporters remembered what he said earlier: "Just think of such a sucker as me as President."

A Money-Saving Suggestion

Little Mike Ryan often sided with the "Gray Wolves," meaning the "boodling" or crooked aldermen of the

1890s. According to a footnote in *Lords of the Levee*, by Herman Kogan and Lloyd Wendt, there was once a proposal to buy six gondolas for the Lincoln Park lagoon.

This time Little Mike Ryan was firmly on the side of fiscal responsibility. He shouted at his fellow aldermen, "Why waste the taxpayers' money buying six gondolas? Git a pair of 'em and let *nature* take its course."

BATHHOUSE & HINKY DINK

"I don't understand it," the Mayor was saying after the elections. "Why did I come out on top in this fight? Everything was against me. Why was it I won?"

And "Bathhouse" John Coughlin replied, "Well, Mr. Mayor, I'd say you won because of the public satisfaction with the well-known honesty which has *caricatured* your every administration!!"

Michael "Hinky Dink" Kenna and "Bathhouse" John Coughlin ruled the notorious, gangster-infested, red-lighted First Ward for almost four decades (1897 to 1938). They made a legendary team. "Bathhouse," so named because he was once employed as a masseur in a bath, was a huge, poetry-spouting, song writing buffoon. "Hinky Dink," named because he was only five feet four inches tall, was the almost-silent, backroom wheeler-dealer. He is known in Chicago history as the man who established the pay rate of 50 cents per vote.

One of Bathhouse's more endearing projects was to build his own zoo on 100 acres he bought near Colorado

Springs in 1902. His zoo featured one of the world's few stolen, alcoholic elephants.

Princess Alice, according to Lloyd Wendt's and Herman Kogan's definitive biography of the duo, titled *Lords of the Levee*, was one of two elephants in Chicago's Lincoln Park Zoo. But Princess Alice had lost part of her trunk in a trap door. Now what taxpayer wants to pay for hay for a defective elephant?

So Princess Alice was crated and shipped to Colorado, where she caught cold in the winter of 1906. Coughlin immediately said that what cured his colds, a little whiskey, could also cure an elephant's elongated sniffles. Princess Alice was given a quart of good whiskey and was quickly cured. Alas, that single experience, that one less-than-gargantuan (for an elephant) taste of demon whiskey made poor Princess Alice into a "confirmed alcoholic," who wandered Coughlin's Zoo Park searching for cowboys with hip flasks. She would actually beg for drinks from them, would swill her liquor as daintily as any elephant could and then would stagger off to go to sleep.

Knowing that he corrupted an elephant did not deter Coughlin from drinking. When the Democratic Convention was held in Denver in 1908, the special Kenna-Coughlin train going there was stocked with "1,000 quarts of champagne, 200 quarts of whiskey, 80 quarts of gin and 12 crates of lemons," according to Finis Farr's *Chicago*. With all those lemons, Hinky Dink and Bathhouse probably hoped to avoid scurvy and other vitamin-deficiency diseases during the long trip to Denver.

Bathhouse is also remembered, albeit with a secretive wince or three, because of his "poetry." His poems included epics titled "She Sleeps by the Drainage Canal," "Ode to a Bath Tub," "Why Did They Build the Lovely Lake So Close to the Horrible Shore," "Two Thirsts with but a Single Drink," "They're Tearing Up Clark Street Again," "Ode to a Lower Birth," and so on. Alas, a tough, heartless reporter for the Chicago Herald revealed that John Kelley, of the Chicago Tribune, was the actual author of many of Coughlin's verses, which he regularly read at City Council meetings.

However, Kelley did not write the verse and song "Dear Midnight of Love." No one but Coughlin could take credit for that song, which received its first (and probably last) week-long performance beginning Oct. 8, 1899. It was a song whose "lyrics . . . conveyed a sense of numbing imbecility," wrote Finis Farr, who was always mean about such things. Judge for yourself. The chorus went as follows:

Dear Midnight of Love,
   Why did we meet?
Dear Midnight of Love
   Your face is so sweet
Pure as Angels above,
   Surely again we shall speak.
Loving only as doves,
   Dear Midnight of Love.

This "famous" Coughlin song was performed before a standing-room-only audience in the Auditorium

Theater by May de Sousa with the help of the Cook County Democratic Marching Club.

Although anyone could accuse Coughlin of writing bad poetry (and many did), every reform organization in Chicago from 1897 onward accused Coughlin and Kenna of corruption. But nothing was ever proven against them.

There was testimony that Coughlin controlled the insurance on the brothels in the Levee and that Bathhouse owned half interest in the one liquor supply house patronized by all the houses in the Levee. Kenna was known to have given free drinks to every bum and drifter who could be imported to the First Ward on election day, but he also provided free lunches to any and all during the depressions of the 1890s.

Bathhouse's and Hinky Dink's most infamous exploit was a party, the First Ward Ball, descriptions of which can still steam the printed page.

What is amazing is that the First Ward Ball took place in the middle of a large and supposedly civilized city in America well into the 20th Century. It stands, even today, as an outstanding example of public debauchery and licentiousness.

The First Ward Ball, termed an "annual underworld orgy" by the Illinois Crime Survey, meant, according to historian Herbert Asbury,

Every harlot, every pimp, every streetwalker and pickpocket, every burglar and footpad was expected to buy at least one ticket, and the keepers of the brothels, saloons and other resorts had to take large blocks. The

most important madames bought boxes, where they sat
in state amidst their strumpets, guzzling champagne by
the case and rubbing elbows with city officials and
prominent politicians . . .

After the 1907 First Ward Ball, the Chicago Tribune
wrote, "If a great disaster had befallen the Coliseum last
night, there would not have been a second story
worker, a dip or pug ugly, porch climber, dope fiend or
scarlet woman remaining in Chicago."

The First Ward Ball merely continued a tradition. For
15 years, ending in 1895, there were parties honoring
Lame Jimmy, a crippled pianist who worked for Carrie
Watson, renowned madam. In reviewing these parties,
Ms. Watson was heard to say that "joy reigned unre-
fined." The joy stopped in 1895 when one drunken
detective shot another cop during the party.

Coughlin and Kenna then took up responsibility for
throwing the wing-dings, which grew larger each year
until the two aldermen were making as much as $50,000
off the parties. In 1907, the Chicago Record Herald
noted that the Chicago Federation of Labor was con-
sidering protesting the fact that waiters *paid* Hinky
Dink and Bathhouse from $3 to $5 for the privilege of
working at the Ball and getting the expected tips.

According to the Chicago Record Herald, the 1907
First Ward Ball featured women in "tawdry costumes of
Egyptian dancers, Indian maidens, geisha girls and
gypsies—all in abbreviated skirts when any were
worn." The men preferred to be "strong men, gladi-
ators, knights of old." By 3 a.m., the party had become

a "drunken debauch. Men and women in maudlin stupors snored and gasped under tables and over chairs. . . . "

By 1908, Bathhouse was ready to begin the Ball with a poem:

On with the dance
Let the orgy be perfectly proper
Don't drink, smoke or spit on the floor
And say keep your eye on the copper.

Some 15,000 people jammed into the Coliseum. Kogan and Wendt described the early hours this way:

The doors of the Coliseum swung open and the tremendous pack outside poured in like a debris-laden flood breaking its gates . . . Some guests, already drunk, sang ribald songs and others bawled out for their favorite ladies of the Levee . . . Women fainted and were passed over the heads of the crowd to the barred exits. "Gangway. Dame fainted!" was the recurring cry.

One newspaper noted that there were so many people inside that drunks might pass out, but they could not fall to the floor, and "fights developed when amorous drunks sought to fondle supposedly helpless women, who defended themselves with hat pins," according to Lords of the Levee.

And all that happened before the queens of the Levee, the madams and their high-priced girls, arrived, and before the Grand March, which was a sight to behold.

Led by Bathhouse John Coughlin, with a lavender cravat and a red sash across his chest, they marched 25 across. Kogan and Wendt wrote, "On they came, madames, strumpets, airily clad jockeys, harlequins, Dianas, page boys, female impersonators, tramps, panhandlers, card sharps, mountebanks and pimps, owners of dives and resorts, young bloods and 'older men careless of their reputations' . . . "

The the party really began, as women draped themselves over the railings and ordered men to pour champagne down their gullets, as young men begged to drink from an Everleigh girl's slipper. "The girls in peekaboo waists, slit skirts, bathing suits, and jockey costumes relaxed and tripped to the floor where they danced wildly and drunkenly . . . Drunken men sought to undress young women and met with few objections . . . Men in women's costumes conducted themselves in a manner described later (by a reformer) as 'unbelievably appalling and nauseating.' "

Despite the fact that 100 policemen were detailed to the party, there were only eight arrests and only one conviction—Bernard Dooley, for trying to enter the building without paying.

Hinky Dink said the party was a "lallapalooza" and added, "Chicago ain't no sissy town."

But the Rev. Melbourne P. Boynton said that if any of the revelers "had a thought of home or their mothers when Auld Lang Syne was sung, such thoughts are choked in the scenes of vice and debauchery which surrounded them."

That 1908 First Ward Ball was the last to qualify for

"Hinky Dink" Kenna and "Bathhouse" John Coughlin (no date).

clergyman condemnation as "a Saturnalian orgy." By 1909, when reform groups were active and strong, the Mayor denied a liquor license to Bathhouse and Hinky Dink. Although 3,000 people came to see a band concert at the Coliseum that year, the life had gone out of the party. Bath and Hink never organized another First Ward Ball.

The end came sadly for both men. Bathhouse John Coughlin died on Nov. 8, 1938, an old, fading, fat alderman, a veteran of 46 years in the City Council, but a man $56,000 in debt because of slow-running horses. Before his death, Bathhouse was finally endorsed by the Municipal Voters' League in 1933 because he "has mellowed with age." Hinky Dink said, "You oughta sue 'em."

Hinky Dink took care of funeral arrangements for Bathhouse. But few people were around to make similar arrangements on Oct. 9, 1946, when Hinky Dink died. "The funeral was a dud," wrote one reporter. After 50 years as boss of Chicago's First Ward, there were only three cars with flowers (Bath had five flower cars). And the Mayor wasn't even there.

But Kenna died a millionaire with an estate probated at $1,003,535, with $426,770 in cash (mostly in $1,000 bills!), plus two pints of 1917 vintage bourbon, 11 suits of long woolen underwear and a 1930 Pierce Arrow limousine.

Toward the end, Hinky Dink never left his suite in the Blackstone Hotel, not even to go to funerals. Very few people attended his funeral, leading one observer to remark, "If you don't go to other people's funerals, they won't go to yours."

The Ultimate Bribe

One of the most successful bribes in the city's history was mentioned in *If Christ Came to Chicago*, written by William T. Stead in 1894.

A railroad was trying to get the right of way to go through the heart of the city. However, one Chicago alderman wasn't offered as much as he thought he was worth for his vote.

The ordinance allowing the railroad to proceed passed the City Council despite the angry alderman's "eloquent and impassioned speech against the tyranny of the railroad corporation," but the measure was then vetoed by the Mayor. A two-thirds majority was needed to pass the ordinance over the veto and every vote would count.

The alderman again threatened to vote against the railroad ordinance unless his price was met.

According to Stead, the alderman then began a

. . . denunciation of the railroad company (during the City Council debate on the veto over-ride) and expressed his strong determination to defend the rights of the people. While he was speaking, the chief of the ring (which was bribing fellow crooked aldermen) laid an envelope before him, on the corner of which was written '$1,000.' Hastily thrusting it into his breast pocket, he continued his speech, when suddenly to the great amusement of those who were in on the secret, he wound up with the declaration that, notwithstanding his detestation of railroad tyranny, and his reluctance to see the streets interfered with, still, under the present circumstances, seeing the great advantages which could accrue from having another depot in the center of the city, he would vote for the ordinance which he had previously opposed.

The measure was passed over the Mayor's veto.

The alderman did not get a chance to look inside the envelope until he went home later that night. He then discovered that it contained only $100! And his vote could not be changed!

The problem with receiving bribes is that you often have to deal with crooks to get the money.

VOTING INFLATION

"Hot Stove" Jimmy Quinn once convinced Honore Palmer, son of millionaire Potter Palmer, to run for alderman. In commenting about that election, Quinn's rival, John F. O'Malley, said, "Damn that feller Quinn! By trotting out that Palmer guy, he raised the price of votes in the 21st Ward from 50 cents to two dollars."

MEET AN HONEST MAN IN CHICAGO POLITICS

By all accounts, George E. Cole was an honest man. That can be said about few men in public life in Chicago's history. Diogenes' lamp would burn out before he found Cole's equal in Chicago.

Cole was a short, thick, tough owner of a printing

shop and stationery store when he was made president of the Municipal Voters' League. He demanded, and got, a free hand.

He waged a long-term, unceasing and usually successful war against local graft and corruption. The Municipal Voters' League motto was "a hundred years ago if men were knaves, why, people called them so." He called the all-powerful traction lord, Charles Yerkes, a "boodler" and a grafter. He demanded the defeat of Hinky Dink Kenna because he was "said to be intimately associated with the gambling element . . . utterly unfit for the position of alderman."

One day the crusader met the people he sought to defeat. Hoyt King, in his laudatory book *Citizen Cole of Chicago*, described the moment when Hinky Dink and Bathhouse John Coughlin, two of the grayest wolves of the City Council, sought a meeting with Cole.

Bathhouse towered over the counter in the MVL office. Hinky Dink had eyes at just about counter level.

"Mr. Cole, I am John J. Coughlin."

"Glad to meet you, Mr. Coughlin."

After the introductions, Bathhouse complained that Cole had done him a "great injustice" in a MVL report which described Coughlin as "Proprietor, Turkish bath establishment; owner of the Silver Dollar; voted for nearly every questionable measure that has come before the Council . . . "

Cole pointed out that the record showed that Coughlin had voted for many questionable ordinances, but Coughlin insisted, "That is not the point, Mr. Cole. In this report, you say I was born in Waukegan. Now,

Mr. Cole, I was born right here in Chicago, and I am proud of it."

Coughlin didn't mind being called a crook, but accusing him of being born outside Chicago was going too far. The newspapers corrected his birthplace the next day.

WHEN TO CALL IT QUITS

There was a war in Chicago from 1916 to 1921 over control of the "bloody 19th" Ward between Johnny Powers, who controlled the corrupt ward since 1888, and Philip D'Andrea, a defrocked priest and ex-convict.

The war began during the 1916 aldermanic contest when the names of those to be eliminated were first posted on Dead Man's Tree in the ward. There were 30 killings before D'Andrea lost.

Even after D'Andrea lost, the bombings, shootings and sluggings continued until two Powers men were murdered in March, 1921. D'Andrea, whose organization was blamed for the assassinations, immediately announced that he was retiring from ward politics.

That didn't help. He was murdered on May 11, 1921. Later two of his buddies swore they would avenge his death. They, too, were murdered.

In Chicago, once you've lost a tough election, it's probably better to get out of town than to stay around and complain.

THINK OF THE MONEY WE SAVED!

"I don't know why I did it. I must have been temporarily insane," said Orville Enoch Hodge.

On another occasion, Hodge said, "If I had to do it over again, I would plead innocent. I was doped up for pain in the stomach. I must not have known what I was doing."

Hodge must have known what he was doing at one time or another. There are varying estimates as to how much he stole from the State of Illinois. Some say it was $2,599,603; others say it was $2,640,878; and no one knows for sure.

Hodge was heading for the Governor's mansion in 1956 when George Thiem, a Chicago Daily News reporter, began breaking stories about Hodge's corruption. Hodge was state auditor when Thiem began examining his vouchers.

Most crooked politicians in Illinois merely overpay contractors and later get secret kickbacks. There was a certain tradition of graft in Illinois. Hodge violated that tradition by cutting out the middleman and, in effect, writing checks directly to himself. It saved time and money, but it led one Republican politician to call Hodge "a likeable jerk."

Among the items Thiem discovered Hodge bought with state funds were: 13 tailor-made shirts for $462.70, two Cadillacs for $9,000, $33,000 for a farm and some registered cows, furnishings for a half-million dollar motel in Ft. Lauderdale, Fla., two airplanes and two motorboats, a pearl necklace and matching earrings for $738, a mink cape for $1,435, a mink stole for $1,904, a hi-fi for $483.19, tickets to Europe for $1,781, plus many smaller items such as "paintbrush, $3.06; soda, $3.59; beer, $6.44; tonic water, $4.20 . . ."

Of the amount taken, $1,571,364 was recovered and Hodge served six years, five months and 11 days in prison. He may have set the record for the most money allegedly taken by a single local public official (although there was the suspicion that he had unnamed help).

But consider the fact that Hodge was doing all this before 1956, when he could buy 13 tailor-made, monogrammed shirts for $462.70, and you might conclude that Illinois taxpayers were probably way ahead on the deal. If he had attempted to buy the same items today, a lot more money might have been misappropriated. That's one unexpected benefit of inflation.

Chapter Four: Businessmen

"If he ran World War I, he could
have made it pay a dividend."
  Said of Samuel Insull

Chicago's moguls have not left a rich lore behind them.

It is, after all, only mildly interesting that Marshall Field I would park his carriage a few blocks from his famed store and walk to work so as not to flout his wealth. Or that Cyrus McCormick, the crotchety millionaire reaper magnate, cut off the coal he had been donating to a minister because the man opposed slavery.

Potter Palmer left a more definite impression than his fellow businessmen, but that's because the man had the heart of a gambler. After the great fire of 1871, he rebuilt the first Palmer House Hotel (which was completed, but hadn't opened, before the fire destroyed it) and claimed his new structure was completely fireproof. In fact, in advertisements, he challenged anyone to light a fire in a locked Palmer House room, which would remain closed for one hour. The ads said, "If at the expiration of that time, the fire does not spread beyond the room, the person accepting this invitation is to pay for all damages done and for the use of the room. If the fire does extend beyond the room (I claim it will not), there shall be no charge for the damage done." No one took him up on his challenge.

But those stories, and the ones you are about to read, are the exceptions. Mostly history presents Chicago's businessmen as single-minded, intellectually rather limited bores. Philip Danforth Armour saying that ministers would preach better sermons "if they included more of Armour's sausages in their diet." Field intoning, "It matters not what a man's income is, reckless extravagance and waste will sooner or later bring him to ruin." Now who didn't know that?

Few of Chicago's wealthy citizens were as giving as Charles Crane, a millionaire who personally financed a study on theater safety after the disastrous Iroquois Theater fire and who left a trust fund for widows and children of his employees.

Other Chicago merchants were not overwhelmingly kind to their employees. The 1911 Vice Commission noted that low wages was a major factor in the number of prostitutes of the day. In addition, Chicago's industrialists were anti-union for generations. After becoming concerned about the labor troubles in the 1880s, Chicago millionaries gave the U.S. Government 632 acres of lakefront property 30 miles from the city. This became Fort Dearborn (donated by the Commercial Club of Chicago), with the Great Lakes Naval Training Station added nearby (given by the Merchant's Club), meaning that local capitalists could call upon either the army or navy or both to protect their interests if labor threatened them.

Most local millionaires were lucky to have arrived in Chicago early, to have staked out an indisputable claim to some part of the town and then to have worked with single-minded intensity for the rest of their lives to amass as much money, property and power as possible. They seldom had time to do much that would be worth retelling.

However, a few of Chicago's businessmen are worth discovering. What follows is an attempt to pierce the balance sheets to find the men.

ALEXANDER HAMILTON HANDLES
ALL OUR WITHDRAWALS

Precious few banks have benefitted from the advice, economic and moral, of Alexander Hamilton, first Secretary of the Treasury of the United States. One Chicago bank claimed that it regularly sought—and received—his advice a half century after his death.

The Bank of Chicago, at 42 S. Clark, was opened by Ira B. Eddy and Seth Paine in the 1850s, and was to be run on strict moral principles. According to Paine's prospectus, this bank would loan no money on real estate because the land belongs to God and cannot be bought or sold. Similarly, no money would be available to "speculators," to anyone "aiding in the making or vending of intoxicating liquors" or to anyone who "slaughtered animals and shed blood for human food." The bank announced that it had no money for and didn't want the following people on the premises: Drinkers of liquors, chewers and smokers of tobacco, eaters of meat, speculators in bread stuffs, and those who owned land or those who loaned money on land.

Oddly enough, despite the fact that nearly everyone in the city (and possibly the nation) was excluded from doing business with the bank, it did rather well until it decided to expand. Paine and Eddy established Harmony Hall in the floor above the bank as a place for spiritualists to gather.

It was bad enough to have a bank which proposed to "do no business which is death to the human body or hell to the soul." But it was too much to have that same bank provide a home for spiritualists. The respectable elements of Chicago decided the bank must go and various businessmen began presenting bills for redemption to the bank, which was issuing its own money in the form of "current bills" (which one critic said were backed by the "pure ether itself").

The bank retaliated. Paine and Eddy called upon the spirit world. "Mrs. Herrick," a medium, went to Harmony Hall, above the bank, entered a trance and, it was said, began speaking with the voice of Alexander Hamilton.

She then came down from Harmony Hall, was installed behind a counter and did business as the "spiritual director" of the Bank of Chicago. Mrs. Herrick/Hamilton ordered who would have their notes on the bank redeemed in U.S. currency and who would not.

The bank closed its doors on Feb. 11, 1853, after considerable criticism from the Chicago business community, and a conservator was appointed for Eddy's estate. We do not know what Alexander Hamilton would have said about that.

THE SOCIAL COUP OF THE 1870s

Perry H. Smith was the vice president of the Chicago & North Western Railroad who knew how to spend his money.

During the 1870s, there had been a bit of rivalry between Mrs. Potter Palmer and others in town as to who would be the social leader of Chicago. On Jan. 2, 1878, when the Smith white marble mansion opened for a housewarming, the Smiths clearly outdid the Palmers.

During the festivities, the Smiths showed their guests to the butler's pantry, certainly an odd place to gather for the purpose of creating a social sensation. Stranger still, the guests were shown the three faucets there—one each for hot water, for cold water and, to round out the necessities, a third for champagne.

THE SIREN OF BATTLE CREEK

Samuel Eberly Gross received the notice of the world both in the middle of his life and just prior to his death.

He was worth between $3,000,000 and $5,000,000 in the 1890s when a dollar went much further than it did today. He got his money by selling Chicago real estate lots and homes. In 1890, he sold up to 500 lots a week. During the 10 years before 1894, the energetic Mr. Gross sold 30,000 lots and built more than 7,000 homes.

He billed himself as the "world's greatest real estate promoter." He advertised easy monthly installments

and low down payments. He was credited with organizing the idea of bringing prospective clients out to a
site for free and offering them lunch. The mind boggles
at what Mr. Gross might have done with Florida swamp
land or the Arizona desert and a little advertising time
on TV!

Gross gave the world a giggle when he entered a
Chicago federal court and accused Edmund Rostand of
plagiarism. Rostand had written "Cyrano de Bergerac"
in the early 1890s, but Gross claimed that "Cyrano" was
stolen from his blank verse comedy, "The Merchant
Prince of Cornville."

After all, Gross reasoned, the leading character in
"The Merchant Prince of Cornville" had a huge nose,
just as Cyrano did. "But," playwright Rostand shouted
during the depositions, "there are big noses everywhere
in the world!"

The world laughed at Gross' suit, but the Chicago
Federal court didn't. A report to the court noted, "The
greatest dramatists have been the most persistent pur-
loiners of the literary property of those less gifted."

Judge Christian C. Kohlsaat decided in favor of
Gross, who left his play at the Port St. Martin Theater
in Paris in 1889 and who contended that Rostand had
access to it there. All royalties were given to the wealthy
Mr. Gross, but he magnanimously refused them.
Because of the legal problems associated with the play,
actor Richard Mansfield could not do the play in
America until the 1920s.

Gross later built Alta Vista, a North Side Chicago

landmark street because it is an exact replica of a London sidestreet.

In its obituary, the unforgiving Chicago Tribune noted that, in 1909, Gross married Miss Ruby Lois Houghey, the daughter of a teaming contractor in Battle Creek, Mich. The wedding occurred less than a month after Gross' wife divorced him. Gross was 66 years old, his bride was but 18. But Gross died bankrupt just four years later.

At this point in time, it does not pay to comment on May-December affairs of the heart.

Before his death, the Tribune noted, Gross' "chief occupation for many months was the dodging of process servers who trailed him day and night until they caught him napping . . . " And this for a man who was worth as much as $5,000,000 four years before.

Upon his death, it was said that he had less than $150,000 to his credit. We do not know if the exertions of his four-year-old marriage to the 18 year-old-siren of Battle Creek speeded his demise.

The Life and Death of the Voluptuary Rapist of Chicago

Charles Tyson Yerkes came to Chicago in the 1880s to rape the town. Even today, we aren't sure who was the raper and who was the rapee.

This street transit mogul began at eight years of age, when he borrowed $18 from his father and made a deal with a local grocer to sell a certain soap to the grocery at nine cents a pound. Little Yerkes bought the soap at six cents a pound, thus starting his fortune.

He was an office boy in a grain commission house at 15, began his own stock brokerage office at 22, started in banking at age 25 and, at age 34, was sentenced to two years and nine months in prison for misapplying the funds of Philadelphia. Part of his troubles were caused by the 1871 Chicago Fire, which created financial problems across the country.

When the Chicago Dispatch newspaper learned of his conviction some years later, he told the editor, Joe Dunlap, "If you publish it, I, myself, personally will kill you, sure!" Another account claimed Yerkes said, "Damn right it's true (that Yerkes went to prison). And you tell that God-damned Dunlap if he ever publishes a line or tells a soul, I'll kill him the first time I see him." Whatever Yerkes said, he was quite thin-skinned about his prison record.

Yerkes was pardoned from prison after seven months. He eventually came to Chicago, allegedly with only $40,000, but he was the secret head of a Philadelphia traction ring. He bought control of the North Chicago City Railway Co. in May, 1886, organized the West Chicago Street Railway Co. two years later and continued to expand. Within a very short time, he was the greatest street railway magnate in the Midwest and a millionaire.

He got that way through a very simple expedient: He bought whatever favors he required from any and very nearly all local politicians.

He was Chicago's ultimate corruptor at a time when

almost everyone in the City Council and local government was ready, willing and anxious to be bought. In
fact, he owned the government and one alderman admitted, "You can't get elected to the (City) Council
unless Mr. Yerkes says so."

Yerkes' bribes paid him well. One critic wrote, "It is
not too much to say that the City Council has given Mr.
Yerkes . . . franchises, tunnels and monopoly rights
which, if put on the market today could not be worth
less than $25,000,000 . . . But we may search the records
of the city treasury from end to end without finding that
the citizens received from him in return five per cent on
the whole of this gigantic sum."

He was often embarrassingly frank, saying, "The
secret of success in my business is to buy up old junk, fix
it up a little and unload it upon some other fellows."
When folks complained that his street trolleys were too
crowded, Yerkes defended squashing commuters,
saying, "It is the straphangers who pay the dividends."

However, we do not really know if he caused local
corruption or merely benefitted from it. After he was
virtually run out of town, he went to London where he
helped create the tube system subway without a hint of
bribery or scandal. It may be that Yerkes, who was
damned by every populist, journalist and crusader of
the 1890s, was more a willing victim of local
immorality. It is a fact that, after he left, Chicago had a
perpetually antiquated but reasonably efficient transportation system, something most other cities didn't
have.

While he was in town, Yerkes was evil incarnate.

Joseph Medill of the Chicago Tribune thundered, "The press of Chicago has no favorable regard or respect for a fellow who uses Chicago as a milch cow, and who takes the butter and cream to New York to be consumed there; who grabs franchises in Chicago and uses their excessive profits to erect a palace in New York crammed with pictures, statuary, bric-a-brac and luxuries of the most costly kind."

Yerkes built a $4,000,000 mansion in New York, had an art collection later sold for $726,200 including a $30,000 portrait of himself, plus paintings by Rembrandt, Rubens, Hals, Corot, Reynolds and Botticelli. He slept in an $80,000 bed which once belonged to the King of the Belgians.

Because of the way he bought his system piecemeal, Yerkes had a different franchise coming up for renewal nearly every year. This meant ever bigger bribes to the City Council, and it meant that long-term bond financing would escape him. As one writer noted, "No one was anxious to buy 30-year bonds from a company which might cease to exist in less than a decade."

So Yerkes attempted to secure his franchises for longer than the then-current 20-year maximum time limit. Say, forever.

In 1895, he tried to get the "Eternal Monopoly" bill (no sense thinking short term!) passed through the state legislature, but Governor Peter Altgeld vetoed it, despite being offered a $500,000 bribe. Afterwards Yerkes said he respected Altgeld, but that didn't stop Yerkes from attempting to bribe others.

Again, in 1897, when a new governor was in power, Yerkes tried to get the Humphrey bills passed. They would have given him 50-year franchises and they, too, failed. Finally, the state legislature passed a law stating that the City Council could give Yerkes longer franchises, an act of good government which cost Yerkes a reported half a million dollars in bribes.

Attention was riveted on the Chicago City Council, a body known throughout the land for its ability to sell itself to the highest bidder.

Yerkes bought the Chicago Inter-Ocean newspaper so it could blast the "trust press"—the Daily News, Tribune, Times, Herald and Post, all of which opposed Yerkes.

The Mayor, Carter Harrison II, said he would eat his brown fedora if Yerkes got his franchises for 50 years. Harrison spoke in every ward in the city, while a confederate flanked him with a noose. The crowds chanted, "Hang 'em, hang 'em," as a threat to any alderman who would side with Yerkes.

But Yerkes fought back. Harrison had correctly described Yerkes as "a fighter, with the heart of a lion, the craft of a fox, the viciousness of a leopard and the watchfulness of a timber wolf guarding her young."

It took a lot of pressure to convince some aldermen. After all, just a few years before, the aldermen created a mythical gas company, the Universal Gas Co., gave the rights to the streets to it, and later sold the non-existent company to its competitor for $175,000. There was money to be made on franchises.

Harrison called in the two most corrupt aldermen in the city's history, the controllers of the Levee red light district. Harrison told Hinky Dink Kenna and Bathhouse John Coughlin that he needed help.

That meeting was the turning point of the controversy and it has often been remembered in Chicago history. In his autobiography, *The Stormy Years*, Harrison recalled that Bathhouse invoked the name of Billie Mason, Congressman at large from Illinois and later a U.S. Senator. Mason was described as "a rolypoly, oleaginous barrel of wind, good humor and bonhomie, a fair lawyer of the criminal school, probably never troubled by a conscience."

"Mason," Bathhouse remembered, "told me: Keep clear of the big stuff, John—it's dangerous. You and Mike stick to the small stuff; there's little risk and in the long run it pays a damned sight more!" Harrison got their votes.

The entire issue of the traction franchises was resolved during a tense, climactic meeting of the City Council on Dec. 19, 1898. Galleries were filled to capacity. Jack Corey, Harrison's associate, was there, dangling his noose from one gallery, in plain view. A North Side German organization, led by a band, was outside playing patriotic songs.

When a photographer exploded a flash, Ald. "Babe" Ballenberg jumped in terror and another alderman said, "Those Dutchies from the North Side just shot an alderman who would not promise to vote right." Ballenberg almost fainted.

The noose, the pressure on Hinky Dink and Bathhouse, the meetings throughout the city, the relentless attacks by George E. Cole and his Municipal Voters' League resulted in a 40 to 23 vote against the Allan Law. Yerkes was denied his long-term franchises. The forces of Good and Truth and Clean Government were victorious for one single, shining day in Chicago history.

Within six months, in June, 1899, Yerkes had sold his holdings and departed for London. But the man couldn't even exit peacefully, and he certainly wasn't forgiven for giving the University of Chicago the finest telescope in the world. The Yerkes Observatory in Lake Geneva, Wisc., was built for the instrument, but journalist-historian Kenan Heise recently wrote:

It was a case of wheeling and dealing for the crafty Yerkes. He was attempting to sell out, and wanted to impress his buyers with his solvency, which had been questioned. The buyers stood ready to use his shaky financial status to put the price down, so Yerkes had his gift announced during the negotiations. But the buyers were unaware of the stipulation in the donation that the money would not be forthcoming for a year.

The scheme may have saved Yerkes several million dollars—he sold his Chicago holdings for almost $26,000,000.

Yerkes died on Dec. 29, 1905, leaving an estate of only $2,100,000, far lower than previous estimates of his net worth. Wayne Andrews in his book, *Battle for Chicago*, wrote, "If this was not a great fortune, it was a good deal of money for anyone to accumulate who never left off having love affairs. At heart a voluptuary, Yerkes was too fond of sofas . . . "

Lloyd Lewis and Henry Justin Smith in *Chicago: The History of its Reputation*, reported that Mr. and Mrs. Yerkes had been separated until the day of his death because of "Mr. Yerkes friendship for a Mrs. Sue Grigsby, a woman of high colored career, and for her daughter Emilie. It was told how the great plunger" (now what did the authors mean by that?) "and connoisseur built a splendid Park Avenue house whose ownership stood in Emilie's name."

Chicagoans can forgive, and possibly forget, private immorality. Public sinning is to be remembered far beyond the grave.

THE FALL OF THE MOST PERFECT TOWN IN THE WORLD

George Pullman began life in Chicago as a hero, a construction engineer of wide renown. He ended life as the town villain and his body had to be protected in its grave lest ghouls kidnap his remains or desecrate his resting place. Only Richard Nixon fell from public esteem more rapidly than did George Pullman.

Back in 1859, Chicago was slowly sinking into the mud. City fathers had begun raising the street levels, which meant that unless local buildings could somehow be lifted off their foundations, jacked up and given new basements, their entrances would lie beneath street level.

George M. Pullman showed how this could be done. His crews would dig ditches alongside the foundations of buildings to be lifted, placing logs on both sides of the lowest walls. Holes would then be cut through the foundation, with logs passing through the holes and resting on the logs placed on both sides of the foundation walls. Then jackscrews would be put under the logs that passed through the foundation. When 6,000 such jackscrews were in place, the 600 men on the crew, each assigned to monitor 10 jackscrews, would be ordered to give each jack a quarter turn. This would slowly raise the building—or the entire block—so a new foundation could be built. Using this method, Pullman raised the Matteson and Tremont Hotels, the warehouses on South Water street and the wholesale stores on Lake Street. It would take up to five days to raise a building or a block and nothing was broken inside the buildings, where business often went on as usual.

Any man who could literally lift entire blocks of buildings out of Chicago's pervasive ooze naturally earned the respect of his fellow Chicagoans.

(Remember, mud was so bad in Chicago that signs were often placed in mud holes in the middle of the streets saying, "No Bottom." There was a story of a man seen with only his head and hat sticking out of the mud. Someone on the sidewalk asked if he needed help and the man answered, "No thanks, I have a horse under me.")

Pullman went on to earn a fortune with the Pullman Palace Car Co. A. T. Andreas, in his polite *History of Chicago* (published in 1885, when everything was more polite) noted that "Pullman has been very generally credited with having originated the sleeping-car. This is not true." What Pullman did was to take a good idea on which other folks were spending only $4,000 per car and decide to spend $18,000 to create a palace on wheels. And that earned him a fortune.

During a time when rail travel was incredibly uncomfortable, Pullman offered luxury. He also brought a firm knowledge of public relations to the field by making sure that Lincoln's body traveled back home from Washington, D.C., in a Pullman Sleeping Car, assuring the car maximum publicity.

But Pullman wanted to be known for more than merely building luxurious railroad cars. So he created his version of a workman's paradise, the village of Pullman, one of the world's first totally planned communities. He wanted to change the psychology of the American working man. His village would make "better workmen by removing from them the feeling of discontent and desire for change which so generally characterize the American workman, thus protecting the employer from loss of time and money consequent upon intemperance, labor strikes and dissatisfaction which generally result from poverty and uncongenial home surroundings." He favored Chicago as the site for his workers' Valhalla because he thought that the breezes off Lake Michigan in the summer would allow his men to work 10 per cent harder than elsewhere.

He spent $5,000,000 creating the town, which was just south of Chicago at the time, but which is now within the city limits. Of course, being a rational industrialist of the 19th Century, Pullman expected a profit on his investment. The town had to net Pullman six per cent a year. The church, built at a cost of $57,000, carried a rent of $3,600 a year and was empty much of the time because no sect could afford to locate there. Pullman allegedly said, "When the church was built, it was not intended so much for the moral and spiritual welfare of the people as it was for the completion of the artistic effect of the scene." The library cost $3 a year for membership, and most of his workers could not afford that.

For about a decade, Pullman received the applause of the world for his town, which was free of beer joints and prostitutes (workers had to sneak out of town, avoiding company spies, to find such pleasures. The only place to serve drinks in town, the Florence Hotel, charged so much that only the rich could afford to go there.) In 1896, the Prague International Hygenic and Pharmaceutical Exposition picked Pullman as the most perfect town in the world.

Perhaps news traveled slowly to Prague in those days. Two years before, in 1894, all hell had broken loose in the Pullman company and in America. And the town was blamed for starting the troubles.

It seems that George Pullman decided he could cut wages during the depression of 1893-94. He could. He was an employer. But he was also a landlord, who insisted that, while cutting wages, his town would continue to earn its six per cent. Stories were circulated of workmen being paid $9.07 for 12 days' labor, with $9 being deducted for rent. That left the chap with only seven cents to feed his family for the next 12 days. One worker testified, "I have seen men with families of eight or nine children crying because they got only three or four cents after paying their rent." The result was a strike. The Pullman workers, George's so-called "children", were rebelling.

Understand that, by 1893, Pullman had created a monopoly. He never sold his sleeping cars. They were leased to the railroads, which gave all overcharges for sleeping accommodations to Pullman. He had over 2,000 cars on 125,000 miles of railroads. His company assets were $62,000,000 and Queen Victoria was one of his stockholders.

There had been a strike in 1882, but the 1,000 men who went out never again worked for Pullman. The same thing happened in 1884 to 150 men protesting a cut in pay and to the 1,400 Pullman workers who demanded the eight-hour day in 1885. When the strike of 1894 was called, Pullman had become the intransigent symbol of an age of anti-unionism.

Not that Pullman had the support of all his fellow capitalists. Mark Hanna yelled, "The damned idiot ought to arbitrate, arbitrate and arbitrate! Oh, hell! Go and live in Pullman and find out how much Pullman gets selling city water and gas 10 per cent higher to those poor fools. A man who won't met his own men halfway is a God-damn fool!"

But Pullman had support where he needed it most— from other railroad owners and from President Grover Cleveland, who said, "If it takes every dollar in the Treasury and every soldier in the United States Army to deliver a postal card in Chicago, that postal card shall be delivered." It was.

It took 14,000 troops to do it, while two-thirds of the country's rail transportation was paralyzed and a dozen people were killed.

Arrayed against Pullman, in addition to his "children," were union leader Eugene V. Debs, who would go to jail for contempt of court; Clarence Darrow, who would quit his job as lawyer for the railroad to defend Debs; Illinois Governor John Peter Altgeld and Chicago Mayor John P. Hopkins, a former Pullman employee. Both Altgeld and Hopkins deplored the use of federal troops in Chicago without their request for them.

The strike was broken. It was, in fact, never officially ended. It merely faded away, as federal troops assured that the trains (under the pretext of guaranteeing the delivery of the mails) would run.

Pullman died on Oct. 19, 1897, three years after the strike. His family was concerned that his final resting place might not be restful at all. There were angry workmen who could never be employed at Pullman again because they had joined the strike. There were also precedents: millionaire A. T. Stewart's body was stolen for ransom and ghouls had tried to steal Lincoln's body.

To protect George Pullman, according to Emmett Dedmon's *Fabulous Chicago*, "A great rectangular pit was dug, 13 feet long, nine feet wide and eight feet deep. A flooring of concrete was laid, strengthened and made solid by bands of expanded metal. The work was done with the utmost care and when completed there was a mass of (steel reinforced) concrete 18 inches thick." The lead-lined casket was lowered into this pit, and the casket was covered with tar paper and asphalt. Later more concrete was poured, "on top of which," according to Dedmon, "a series of heavy steel rails were laid at right angles to each other and bolted together. The steel rails were then embedded in another layer of concrete" hiding them from view. The area was sodded and a small headstone was set down in the Pullman family plot in Graceland cemetery. Outwardly, Pullman's grave looks like almost all others in any cemetery in America.

If there is to be a Resurrection, Pullman might have some difficulties getting through all that steel, concrete and asphalt. Judgement Day might have come and gone while a great knocking and rapping is still heard beneath that simple Pullman headstone.

THE HUMAN ICICLE

If ever there was a hero-businessman in Chicago, it should have been Aaron Montgomery Ward, the mail-order millionaire. But he wasn't a hero when he was alive and people have mostly forgotten him since his death.

Around 1890, he yelled at his attorney, George P. Merrick, "Merrick, this is a damned shame! Go and do something about it."

Ward had built an eight-story skyscraper at Michigan and Madison Streets. Across the street from his property, he could see stables, shacks, garbage, circus litter, rotting freight cars and an armory regularly rented for prize fights, wrestling matches and masquerade balls featuring local prostitutes dressed as harem girls. All this was on the precious lake front.

Ward wanted the property cleaned up and, according to Lois Wille's excellent book, *Forever Open, Clear and Free*, he began a 20-year battle to keep the lake front available to parks, beaches and citizens. It cost him, she estimated, $50,000, or more than $200,000 in today's money, to win his fight. He filed the first of four lawsuits in 1890. By 1897, the Illinois Supreme Court upheld Ward, despite one alderman saying that the downtown lakefront "is no place for a park."

The court ordered that all buildings on the lakefront east of Michigan Avenue be removed unless all adjacent property owners would agree that they could stay. The famed Art Institute stands where it does today only because the husband of one property owner, Mrs. Sarah Daggett, forged her signature on the petition allowing it to remain. The courts then upheld a husband's right to do that.

Ward fought against a new armory being built on the lakefront, regretted that he didn't demand the removal of the Art Institute, and battled in court against a museum on the lake front. Local newspapers called him "stubborn," "undemocratic" and "a human icicle," but he continued to fight for what he thought was right.

Finally, in 1909, the Illinois Supreme Court once again upheld Ward. The ocean fronts near the center of

New York, Los Angeles and San Francisco are given over to commercial uses. Chicago's lake front, directly opposite its most valuable commercial land, contains a park, a marina, and a glorious fountain. Our lakefront is a thing of beauty because of A. Montgomery Ward.

Before his death, Ward said of his accomplishment:

Had I known in 1890 how long it would take me to preserve a park for the people against their will, I doubt if I would have undertaken it. I think there is not another man in Chicago who would have spent the money I have spent in this fight with the certainty that even gratitude would be denied as interest. I fought for the poor people of Chicago, not the millionaires . . . . Here is park frontage on the lake, comparing favorably with the Bay of Naples, which city officials would crowd with buildings, transforming the breathing spot for the poor into a showground for the educated rich. I do not think it is right . . . Perhaps I may yet see the public appreciate my efforts. But I doubt it.

A few people appreciate what Ward did. A few.

THE LARGEST FINANCIAL COLLAPSE IN CHICAGO HISTORY

Samuel Insull's life was pure Horatio Alger filtered through a Greek tragedy.

During the Roaring '20s the companies he headed were worth between $3 and $4 billion! His personal fortune was about $150,000,000. He controlled most of the electricity and gas and many of the railroads in the

Midwest. He threatened to buy and sell entire political parties and, given enough time, he might have purchased the Presidency for some lucky man, who would have been required to love electricity and electrical companies.

His downfall was complete and ultimately tragic. It was almost as if the Gods sought absolutely to prove that what They gave They could swiftly take away.

Insull had learned Pittman shorthand at age 14, a talent which eventually allowed him to assist the English representative of the Thomas A. Edison Co. Sam Insull operated the first telephone switchboard in England, with George Bernard Shaw as his battery boy.

He went to America in 1892, was Edison's personal secretary, supervised the Edison manufacturing plant in Schenectady, N.Y., and, after General Electric was formed—and Edison's family relegated the ambitious Insull to a second vice presidency—he came to Chicago.

Insull's career in Chicago was meteoric. He was a bold, bribing risk-taker. For instance, Insull demanded that a turbine capable of generating 5,000 watts of power be built for the Chicago Edison Co.

Insull recalled, "When they turned on the steam, my friend Mr. Sargent (the chief consulting engineer) told me that he thought I had better get back to the office on Adams St. The 'innards' of the turbine were scraping on the casing and making a terrible noise." The engineer, it seemed, wasn't sure if the turbine, the largest ever built at that time, would blow up or not.

But Insull insisted on standing by, saying, "Well, Sargent, if it blows up, the company will blow up, and I will blow up, too; so I might as well stay here, and between us we will finish the job."

The generator didn't blow up, it worked and, for a long time, so did everything Insull touched. He was the organizer, the man who could get things done.

He took over several suburban electric companies, created the Public Service Co. of Northern Illinois and, within two years, was providing 24-hour-a-day dependable electric power, where before there was only sporadic daytime service. He spent $11 million on plants to supply power to Chicago transit systems *before* they committed themselves to buying it from him. He took over the Chicago, Aurora and Elgin, the Chicago North Shore and Milwaukee Railway, and the Chicago, South Shore and South Bend Railroads, and in short order made them profitable.

He was named chairman of the Illinois State Council of Defense during World War I and, with a budget of a tenth of what similar groups had in other parts of the country (only $50,000), he raised $300,000 for the war while spending none of his budget. He did that through a patriotic cookbook (profit: $15,000), selling seed corn (profit: $150,000) and other notions. Folks said that if Insull had been running the war he "could have made it pay a dividend."

By 1926, when Insull was 67, he could drive through the countryside around Chicago, look back, watch the lights of the city go on, and know they were all supplied with power from his companies.

By 1929, he was president of 15 corporations, the chairman of 56 and a member of the board of 81. According to *Insull* by Forrest McDonald, a most definitive book on this amazing man, Insull's dizzying empire had 600,000 stockholders; 500,000 bondholders; more than 4,000,000 customers; produced an eighth of all the electricity and gas consumed in America, and "probably as much as the total consumed by any other nation on earth."

Among his companies, Commonwealth Edison, delivering electricity to Chicago, was worth $400,000,000; Peoples Gas, which gave gas to Chicago, was worth $175,000,000; Public Service of Northern Illinois, which supplied gas and electricity to 300 towns around Chicago, was worth $200,000,000, and there were railways, utility companies which sold gas, water, ice and heat in 4,000 towns in Maine, New Hampshire, Vermont, New York, New Jersey, Pennsylvania, Delaware, Maryland, Virginia, West Virginia, North Carolina, Georgia, Florida, Alabama, Tennessee, Louisiana, Mississippi, Texas, Oklahoma, Arkansas, North and South Dakota, Indiana, Illinois, Wisconsin, Michigan and Ontario, Canada.

Insull was happiest delivering power and manipulating companies. He didn't drink and seldom shook hands. He did not jest and was seen by many as a colorless gnome. He was a short, boring man whose personal life was in a shambles. His actress wife was an unhappy, unfulfilled woman, who tried and failed to make a stage comeback based upon his millions. He built Chicago's Lyric Opera House, a gigantic shoebox for culture, partially to make her happy and partially to gain a place for himself in high society.

But he did answer his own phone at home when his customers complained, a trait which should make up for many failings and should make him a hero for generations to come. (There were fewer phones then, so this trait makes him a minor, rather than a major, hero.)

Every time Insull left town for a rest, his empire tottered.

Insull got his first taste of what was to come in 1926. During a rough Senatorial campaign between Frank L. Smith and William McKinley, an Insull enemy, Insull sent a cable to his underlings giving them carte blanche in the campaign. As a result $172,925.19 of electric company funds went to Smith. When Julius Rosenwald, of Sears Roebuck, heard of this, he offered Smith a bribe of $550,000 (10,000 shares of Sears stock) if he would withdraw. As you can see, being a political candidate in Illinois can sometimes yield dividends. In this case, there was a Senate investigation and Smith was never allowed to take his seat. (That was the second time in Illinois history that happened—Sen. William Lorimer had been expelled from the Senate a decade earlier on similar grounds.)

However, when it came to political bribery and wheeling and dealing, the Smith money was peanuts. There was, for instance, the notorious Ogden Gas Company incident, during which a group of Chicago aldermen and political dealers created a mythical company, distributed stock amongst themselves and awarded their company a better franchise than was given to Insull's Peoples Gas Light and Coke Co. Ogden Gas sold its rights to Peoples Gas for $7,333,333 and each political sharpster involved profited to the tune of $666,666.

It should also be noted that Insull wasn't always there for the taking. In 1897, some alderman created a phony electric company titled Commonwealth Electric, which was given a 50-year franchise to operate in Chicago. They then went to Insull and demanded to be bought off. But he didn't offer them a cent. The reason: Insull had secured the rights to buy "the electrical equipment of every American manufacturer. Commonwealth could hold its franchise for eternity but could never light a single bulb," according to Insull biographer Forrest McDonald. Insull bought the Commonwealth franchise for $50,000.

He also bought politicians and his generosity usually paid off. During the 1900s, Insull got a deal whereby he could operate North Shore trains over the city of Chicago elevated tracks for $50 per year per car. Insull made over $3,000,000 on that little favor alone.

One writer in the magazine The Nation noted, "Insull was responsible for the degradation of municipal government to its lowest level of corruption and in-competence."

That may be so, but in 1931, banks were willing to lend money to Insull, but not to the city of Chicago. A banker was asked during City Council Finance Com-mittee hearings, "Do you mean to tell me that the credit of the city of Chicago is not as good as that of Samuel Insull?" The reply was, "Exactly that." But that situ-ation was to change rapidly.

The Depression was beginning to hurt Insull.

Although his stocks held up better than most, they were beginning to wilt in value. Suddenly, during a trip to Europe, Insull cabled his son, authorizing him to raise $50,000,000 to support Insull stocks. That money would prove his undoing.

But Insull needed the cash. With investments worth only $20,000,000, Insull controlled properties worth more than $400,000,000. He could be that badly leveraged as long as the securities used as collateral for his bank loans were worth more than the loans. Then the bankers wouldn't get nervous. As the market fell, the securities became worth less than Insull's loans and the bankers demanded more money to cover their loans.

Cyrus Eaton, the mogul, stood in the wings. He had been quietly buying Insull securities and he knew Insull was paranoid about Eaton's goals. During a key moment, when Insull stock prices continued to fall, Eaton threatened to dump his shares on the market. That would collapse Insull's stocks and his empire. To prevent Eaton from carrying out his threat, Insull paid Eaton $40,000,000. Eaton's shares never went on the market, but the end was near for Insull.

The Chicago bankers allowed their New York counterparts to examine the Insull empire and what they found amazed them. From 1912 to 1920, expenses were considered assets under the bizarre Insull bookkeeping. One economist said, "By the same reasoning, one would be entitled to consider the expenses of moving from one house to another as an addition to the value of the furniture."

There was more legerdemain on the books, but even that might not have ultimately brought Insull down. Insull securities were doing well compared to the rest of the market, but they were going down, down, down. The decline was helped by rumors—Insull committed suicide, Insull was seen leaving a New York bank in tears, Insull's mind had snapped, Eaton was winning his battle with Insull.

Insull had various weapons in his fight, but he refused to use them. As the stock went down, his advisers told him to buy short. That is, when the stock was at $300, to sell shares at $295. Then when the stock went down to, say, $270, buy it again and repeat the process. If 20,000 shares were sold at $295, but were bought back at $270, $25 a share could be realized and $500,000 could be made. Fred Scheel, Insull's security salesman, said, "Well, if New York is crazy enough to keep on fighting, we'll end up with all the money and the market will slide to nothing." He also advised against buying the companies' own shares to shore up the market, saying, "You can't go on buying your own stocks forever. Sooner or later you run out of money."

But that's what Insull decided to do. All Insull employees were told "sell stocks if you want to hold on to your job."

But that didn't work either. The price of his stocks— and his empire—crumbled and finally the New York banks were able to force him out.

It happened on July 5, 1932. Throughout the day, directors of all his companies gathered and watched as

Insull officially resigned. The exit of Samuel Insull took a full day, with reporters in an outer room noting who left and in what emotional state they were.

During the day, his country estate, the furniture, his cars and even the family silverware were taken from him. When he finally left, he only had an $18,000 a year pension for his 40 years with his companies. He said, "Here I go, gentlemen, after 50 years, a man without a job."

Others were worse off. Clerks, salesmen, janitors and thousands of others who believed in Insull and his companies crashed with him. A retired contralto, Augusta Lenska, who owned Insull stock, tried to commit suicide by throwing herself in front of a street car.

Then came the accusations and indictments, with Insull escaping from Chicago to Canada to London to Paris to Turin to Milan to Salonika, where he almost succeeded in re-creating his empire. Insull made a survey of electrical power development in Greece and, if the dictator there had won the election of 1933, Insull would have become a citizen and would have been minister of electric power in the cabinet. But Gen. Gondylis lost by 700 votes and America wanted Insull back to face trial(s).

The former czar of electricity and gas stood trial in 1934 for using the mails to defraud. There would be other trials and the verdict on Insull and all of his associates would always be the same: Not guilty.

During the first trial, which lasted six weeks, the jurors decided that Insull was innocent five minutes after they locked the world behind them. According to McDonald, the jurors thought it wouldn't look proper if they re-appeared in court just five minutes after they left it. So, because one of them was having a birthday that day, they ordered a cake, celebrated, and whiled away the time until their entrance would be more seemly.

Insull never did stage a comeback. He tried, in 1936, to form a network of radio stations, but the local advertising wasn't there and the plan faded.

Then, in 1938, a French police report said, "An un-identified man was found in a state of collapse on the platform of the Tuileries subway station near the Place de la Concorde. He was neatly dressed in a gray suit with red stripes, wore a brown felt hat and had 7 francs, 7 centimes (about 35 cents) in his pocket. He was of medium size with white hair. He had no identification papers, but the initials 'S.I.' were on his handkerchiefs and underclothing. Agent 2023."

His estate was valued at $1,000. His debts: $14,000,000.

When it was all over, one historian would write, "Insull made a substantial contribution to the great Depression; he was probably not a thief in the sense that a burglar was a thief, but essentially only a crashing bore, who numbed people's brains with his incessant ciphering and figuring. A rational society would have entrusted Insull with nothing more important than reading the gas meters." (*Chicago*, Finis Farr).

Some people in Chicago may have forgotten Samuel Insull. Those who remember won't forgive.

Chapter Five: Gamblers and Gangsters

"There's a sucker born every minute."
Mike McDonald, 1873

Chicago's gamblers and gangsters left a legacy the city didn't appreciate. Wherever a Chicagoan goes on this earth, as soon as he or she identifies the city he or she is from, most foreign nationals will cradle a pretend machine gun in their arms and go "ratta-tat-tat."

And Chicagoans are ashamed of that reputation. The site of the St. Valentine's Day Massacre has been torn down, gangster tours have progressively less to show because old people's homes and empty lots replace Chicago's formerly sinful places, and generally speaking a Chicagoan would rather show off his or her lake front than the last place where a gangster was found in the trunk of a car. (Nowadays that's either under Wacker Dr. or out at the O'Hare parking lots, and neither is much to look at anyway.)

Chicago's gamblers were a colorful lot, and many of them were of Southern heritage. However, the professional full-time gambler, owner of a wide-open saloon with roulette and poker, has gone the way of the passenger pigeon (or the alderman who doesn't own a three-piece suit). Gamblers in Chicago today are a furtive lot, horse bettors and sleazy sellers of football parlay cards—hardly the people to tell tales about.

Chicago's gangsters began as organizational geniuses, folks who could use muscle and the ability to bribe everyone in sight as a method of furthering their businesses, which included selling human flesh (prostitution), gambling, battling Prohibition, and so on. During Prohibition, they were heroes, the men who were justly fighting stupid laws to provide the public with what it wanted.

Gradually, the gangsters began to change. Their methods grew more harsh. They became greasier, more pig-like, more brutal, uncivilized.

By the time Al Capone took over Chicago's mobs, muscle was the rule. Enforcers were enlisted, and they could and did hang men on meathooks while jabbing them with cattle prods. Often victims owed the syndicate "juice," or loans to be repaid at impossibly high interest rates.

William "Action" Jackson was hung on a meathook for two days while he was tortured with icepicks, baseball bats, blowtorches and cattle prods. Anthony "Lover" Moschiano was stuffed into a car's trunk where he was repeatedly stabbed in the neck.

The romance, the adventure, the idea of being just slightly outside the law, taking money from people who wanted to lose it, gambling on the cards or the roll of dice, consorting with energetic ladies with wicked reputations, had completely changed. The torturer, the terrorist, the person who could squeeze a few bucks in protection from honest shopkeepers, the tough guy who could invade legitimate businesses because of threats to the owner's wife or children, entered the scene.

Such people are beneath contempt. They are still around, some folks in Chicago society still fawn over them, and because of the generations of accommodations between the Chicago political structure and organized crime, local gangsters are often immune from all retribution—except from their own kind.

The shift from the fascinating crook to the brutal hoodlum happened gradually, but Al Capone fully embodied the New Brutality. And that is where the story telling will stop. Tales of men hung on meat hooks only make heroes of the disgusting.

A SMALL ROGUES GALLERY
OF THE SOMEWHAT INFAMOUS

We begin with thumbnail sketches of a few of the more interesting criminals in Chicago history:

• Eddie Jackson was the most expert pickpocket of all time, according to historian Herbert Asbury. Jackson kept an attorney on retainer and reported to his lawyer each hour. If an hour passed without Jackson showing up, the shyster knew his client was in jail somewhere and it was time to bail him out. Jackson was arrested 2,000 times, was convicted only twice and served only a year and 10 days in jail.

• Con Brown was known as the Prince of the Bounty Jumpers during the Civil War. With enlistments worth as much as $400 apiece, Brown was quite patriotic. He joined 20 different military units during the first three years of the Civil War. He got more patriotic while in prison—during his five escapes from local jails, he joined three different regiments.

• Terry Druggan and Frankie Lake, two beer runners, were sentenced to jail during the 1920s, but they didn't spend much time there. Druggan spent a lot of time with his wife at home when he was supposed to be in prison, while Lake got out of jail 21 days before he finished serving his sentence. It was rumored that their favored treatment was due to some money changing hands. The sheriff spent 30 days in jail (not his own) for Druggan's and Lake's escapades, while his warden got four months.

• Johnny Rafferty often told newspapermen, "I love a good thief." When a local newspaper called him a crook in 1903, he was so upset he told reporters that he had never "gouged out an eye, cut off a goat's tail, beaten a policeman, held up a train or bitten off a bulldog's nose." Chicago's bulldogs were grateful.

• Newspaper reporters, no matter what they wrote, have usually been immune from gangster retribution. There was at least one exception. Jake Lingle, a Chicago Tribune reporter, was gunned down on June 9, 1930, after which the Tribune offered $25,000 for the name of the killer. The reward was quietly dropped when the Tribune learned that Lingle had been doing very well for a $65 a week reporter. He had a suite in a downtown hotel, a West Side home and a Wisconsin summer home. He wore tailor-made suits, English shoes and had a $100,000 account with his stock broker. It was whispered that he lost $25,000 of the syndicate's money on the stock market, and that he had the temerity to tell The Boys that they "can't touch a newspaperman." They could. They did.

• Hymie Weiss vowed to avenge the murders of the seven Bugs Moran followers in the St. Valentine's Day Massacre. Instead, he was shot down on the steps of Holy Name Cathedral. The machine gun bullets tore up the building's cornerstone, but it has since been repaired.

• Machine Gun McGurn was arrested, but never convicted, for the St. Valentine's Day Massacre. He often said, "All I did was supply a demand (for booze) that was pretty popular" and "Nobody's on the legit." Seven years after the St. Valentine's Day Massacre, McGurn was shot and killed in a local bowling alley. The murderers left a Valentine behind. It said:

You've lost your job, you've lost your dough;
Your jewels and cars and handsome houses!
Things could be worse, you know—
At least you haven't lost your trousas.

The rhyme definitely demonstrates the deficiency of English literature and poetry courses in the Chicago public schools.

CHICAGO'S FIRST CRIMINALS:
A VAGRANT AND A THIEF

The vagrant was a man named Richard Harper, and his name appears in the city's first directory, followed by his profession—"Loafer."

Harper was arrested in 1833 under Illinois' strict laws, which stated that a vagrant should be sold as an indentured servant. Harper was thus the first man to spend a night in the town's first jail, after which, over the protests of many citizens, he was put up for sale.

No one wanted to bid on the white man. Finally, George White, the black town crier, bought Harper for a quarter. White men went cheaply in those days.

Harper was led away at the end of a chain, but White, a black man, freed Harper, a white man. White's good deed was quickly repaid when, after being arrested for not having papers proving he was a free man, he was given a certificate of freedom. Without that, he might have lost his freedom.

Chicago's first thief was known only as "John Doe." A man named Hatch shared a bunk with "John Doe" in the Wolf Tavern, splitting the 12½ cent lodging rate in 1833. When Hatch got up, he discovered that his entire fortune was gone.

Hatch got an arrest warrant issued for "John Doe," who was arrested by Constable Reed. The jail, which was built in time to house Harper, hadn't been constructed yet, so Reed had to stay awake all night guarding "John Doe" in Reed's carpenter shop.

The trial was held in the Wolf Tavern, either because

the scene of the crime might lead to truth telling or because there were few other structures in town. Over "John Doe's" lawyer's strenuous objections, the defendant was stripped in court, possibly the first strip search in Chicago history and certainly a moment to remember in the annals of local jurisprudence. The stolen money was found wadded in the toe of "John Doe's" sock.

"Doe" was found guilty, but demanded a new trial. It was to be held the next day, but Constable Reed had already lost one night's sleep. He was not about to lose another. Reed let "John Doe" go free on the promise that "Doe" would stick around for the trial.

"John Doe" was never seen in the Chicago area again.

HYMAN, TRUSSELL AND THE LADIES WHO LOVED THEM

Cap Hyman, a local gambler, would, when under the influence of overmuch drink, shoot anything and everything in sight. This deficiency of character led the Chicago Tribune to comment that "the practice of shooting people upon the most trifling provocation is becoming altogether too prevalent in this city."

Another gambler, George Trussell, was his enemy. When both were drunk, they would shoot at each other at sight. They never wounded each other, although their attempts shattered many bar mirrors and shot down many street signs.

In 1862, Cap Hyman lurched into the Tremont House, comandeered the entranceway on Dearborn St., and held the entire hotel as hostage. He fired several shots and refused to allow anyone to enter or leave the hotel, until Police Captain Jack Nelson appeared. Hyman then meekly surrendered, saying, "Jack can shoot too quick for me." Hyman may have been a drunk, but he was not a fool.

His sworn enemy, Trussell, came to a bad end in 1866, and that event directly affected Hyman's future. Trussell was described as "tall, straight as an arrow and (a man who) might have stood as a model for one of Remington's Indian-fighting cavalry officers." Trussell had a mistress named Mollie Cosgriff, also known as Irish Mollie or Mollie Trussell, although she never benefitted from a marriage ceremony. Mollie loved Trussell and he loved Dexter, the most famous trotting horse of the day.

On Sept. 4, 1866, Mollie planned a dinner celebrating the opening of the Chicago Driving Park racing season, during which Dexter and his owner, Trussell, expected to win many a race.

However, Trussell didn't show up at Mollie's planned gala. She found him around 10 p.m. that evening at Wright's saloon. She was wearing, according to the Chicago Tribune, "a gorgeous white moire dress, with a light shawl thrown over it . . . as if she had just come from a dancing party." Mollie was angry. Trussell was standing at the bar listening to a song when his true love approached. He told her to go home.

Mollie shot Trussell once in the side as he stood at the bar, again as he ran away and a third time as he dodged into a livery stable.

Mollie then threw herself on his body and screamed, "Oh, my George! My George! He is dead." Another account stated that she cried, "George! Have I killed you? Have I killed you?" A third reporter wrote that she said, "Oh, George, I would not have shot you if you had not hated me so." However, this book will not dwell overlong on the exact words spoken by Mollie Cosgriff over the body of George Trussell in Prince's Livery Stable on Sept. 4, 1866. History has a lot of better things to do.

Trussell died and Mollie entered a plea of "temporary emotional insanity." She was found guilty of man-slaughter, was sentenced to one year in prison and was pardoned by the governor.

Trussell's estate included five gold watches, two diamond pins, five hats and twelve pair of "cassimere pantaloons."

The entire event started "Gentle Annie" Stafford thinking. She was Cap Hyman's mistress and was known as the fattest brothel keeper in Chicago. Whenever she would ask Cap to marry her, as Mollie so often had asked Trussell, Cap would chuck her many chins and change the subject.

On the afternoon of Sept. 23, 1866, Gentle Annie Stafford entered Cap Hyman's gambling house at No. 81 Randolph Street. She went into his office, dragged him down the stairs and then chased him up Randolph Street. To add to the indignity and to make sure Cap kept up a lively pace, Gentle Annie pursued him with a long rawhide whip.

It was the strangest—and most successful—wedding proposal in Chicago history. Cap and Annie were married a few weeks later, proving that love will find a way.

Their wedding day coincided with the opening of the Sunnyside, a tavern just out of town and newly leased by the nuptial couple. Opening night (and their wedding night) was an evening to remember.

The invitation list, according to the Chicago Tribune, was "select, embracing chiefly the women keepers of some of the more fashionable brothels and those who contribute most liberally to their support."

Cap, who it was rumored had a college education, supervised the party and invited journalists to make sure the moral tone of the event would be quite high. Sleighs brought men from the Board of Trade and the guest of honor, Capt. Jack Nelson, who had arrested Hyman in the Tremont Hotel just four years before.

Gentle Annie, now the new Mrs. Hyman, made sure that the ladies behaved. One "strumpet" claimed she knew all the correct social graces and only repeated a single line throughout the evening, "Who's your favorite poet? Mine's Byron."

The women were introduced, engagement cards were presented and decorum was observed until most of the newspapermen left. Then one woman reflected upon the character of another and a free-for-all resulted. Cap Hyman shot out the lights, the madams began passing out business cards to prospective customers, and various strumpets began doing business in the sleeping quarters upstairs.

During the free-for-all, one lady had "her nose

changed from pug to Roman," the Tribune reported, while another had her face "left in the condition of dissolving views, the red, white and blue each striving to be the predominant color."

The Sunnyside closed six months after the gala opening because of financial problems. Following a mental and physical breakdown, Cap died in 1876, but Gentle Annie continued to run a whore house in Chicago until about 1880.

The story of Gentle Annie's life is that she was able to learn from others. Mollie shot her man and lost him; Annie whipped her man and won him.

THE MAN BEHIND THE STORE

As a gambler and political boss of Chicago in the 1880s, Mike McDonald couldn't have been all bad. After all, he contributed three phrases which have stayed with us ever since.

He built a huge, nearly square-block, four-story gambling establishment known as the Store. Just before it opened in 1873, his partner asked if it was too large and Mike answered, "Don't worry about that. There's a sucker born every minute." That phrase became a movie title and has been quoted by luncheon speakers ever since.

Legend has it that McDonald was also the first man to say, "Never give a sucker an even break."

He was also notorious for the following quip, which became a standard vaudeville routine. McDonald loathed the police. A man came to him and asked for $2.

"What's it for?" asked McDonald.

"Well, we're burying a policeman."

"Fine," Mike is supposed to have said, "here's $10. Bury five of them."

McDonald did more than merely say memorable things. When he came to Chicago at the age of 15, he was already an accomplished card dealer and salesman of half empty candy boxes on railroad trains. During the Civil War he had another racket—enlisting in the army. There were bounties paid for such enlistments from which McDonald would get a commission. McDonald's men would enlist, desert and enlist again, gaining more commissions for the boss. If the Civil War had continued much longer, the North might have had no men in the field, but McDonald might have had a lot of money.

One of McDonald's gambling establishments burned in the Chicago Fire of 1871, but he was able to rebuild quickly (there are those who say that the first structures to be rebuilt after the fire were the whore houses and gambling joints). His profits from a single West Side gambling house were said to be over $100,000 a year, which allowed him to go into politics.

McDonald backed Harvey D. Colvin, a gambler who was also the general agent for the United States Express Co. Colvin ran as a liberal "Law and Order" candidate, again proving that nice words do not a great candidate make.

During his comical and wide-open administration, the king of the Hawaiian Islands, David Kalakua, visited Chicago. Colvin spent much of the day trying to communicate with the king in sign language and gestures before learning that His Majesty spoke fluent English.

By the end of Colvin's term, there were two Mayors of Chicago because of an incredible legal snafu. The mayoralty election had been changed from fall to spring and the City Council passed an ordinance calling for the election of city officers, but never mentioned the office of Mayor. The Council tried to rectify that, but the motion for a special Mayoral election was defeated. So Colvin said that, because no election had been officially called, he could stay in office. And he did.

But that didn't stop others from holding an election. A meeting was held and Thomas Hoyne was nominated. He was "elected" on April 18, 1876, receiving 33,064 votes. Only 749 votes were cast against him.

But Colvin refused to step down despite the fact that Hoyne was sitting in the old City Hall demanding to be recognized as Mayor. Eventually the Circuit Court ruled that Colvin was Chicago's one and only Mayor despite the fact that by the time the City Council had recognized Hoyne as its presiding officer.

Meanwhile, nothing stayed gambler Mike McDonald from his appointed path. The Store flourished with, according to a newspaper of the day, "the most expert manipulators of cards that ever dealt a second or shifted a cold deck . . . "

In those days, McDonald ran Chicago, taking a tariff on everything stolen, on all gambling proceeds and on all profits from prostitution and blackmailing. Of the take, 40 per cent went to the thief or panderer, and 20 per cent went to the police, with the remainder going to McDonald for other bribes.

His control of the town was absolute. Twice a year, phony raids were conducted on the Store, with Mike's permission, so the newspapers could have their headlines. Every once in a while McDonald would exercise his political muscle by having an honest cop demoted. For instance, in 1880 the Store was raided by Police Superintendent Simon O'Donnell. It was an honest raid and for his efforts O'Donnell was relegated to a captaincy and was given the toughest assignments for the rest of his years on the force.

The Store was a gathering place for some of the most colorful crooks in Chicago history. According to *Gem of the Prairie*, by Herbert Asbury, if you went there and stayed in McDonald's wife's boarding house on the upper floors, you might meet Red Jimmy Fitzgerald, who swindled $7,000 from a famous diplomat; Hungry Joe Lewis, who took Oscar Wilde for several thousand dollars; Tom O'Brien, king of the bunko men; and McDonald's one-armed brother-in-law and dice expert, Nick Hogan, who was described by police thus: "If he had two arms he'd have all the money in the world."

During the 1894 World's Fair in Chicago, McDonald's profits from the Store were over $100,000 a month.

In addition to gambling, the Store featured Chicago's oldest bartender, Old Pat Casey, whose saloon once sold Old Casey's Number Six, a whiskey so powerful it was guaranteed to turn the men of Volunteer Fire Company No. 6 into fearless firefighters and battling brawlers. The County Commissioners would often be seen in the Store, leading Old Pat to say, "All they're good for is to sell cheap wine to."

One of McDonald's better swindles was of the city of Chicago. He got the city and county to award him a contract to paint the court house with "a secret preserving fluid." The bill for the job was $128,250 and half the money was paid before the Chicago Daily News discovered that the so-called secret fluid was only chalk and water. It was also learned that William J. McGarigle, the man who succeeded Simon O'Donnell as police chief, handed the $14,000 in bribes to the aldermen and county commissioners in exchange for their votes. McGarigle was convicted of bribery, but he escaped to Canada and didn't return to Chicago for 22 years. McDonald wasn't prosecuted.

Despite his decades of success in gambling, politics, bribing and bossing the underworld, McDonald died an unhappy man. An honest Mayor, John A. Roche, took office in 1887, forcing McDonald to turn over his wife's boarding house to an astrologer and the Store to another gambler. With the $2,000,000 he had accumulated, he bought a newspaper, the Chicago Globe, and ran it for two years. He helped build the city's first elevated railway, sold stone and gravel to the city, and was on his way to becoming as honest a man as he could be.

Then his wife Mary ran away with an actor and minstrel singer named Billy Arlington. The McDonalds got back together again, only to have Mary run away with a second man, the Rev. Joseph Moysant, assistant rector of the Catholic Church of Notre Dame.

McDonald renounced Catholicism, divorced his wife, and married Dora Feldman. She was 23 and a former playmate of McDonald's children. He was 49. Then she shot artist Webster Guerin in 1907. After the murder, she told police that Guerin had been her lover and that she hated McDonald.

McDonald died six months later and, they said, went back to the Catholic Church on his death bed. He also said that his first wife, Mary, was his only true wife. Mary later told reporters she never eloped with either the actor or the rector. She left because of McDonald's "unbearable cruelty."

Despite being his one true wife, Mary got nothing from the McDonald estate. Dora got a third, plus $40,000 for a defense fund. She was acquitted of the Guerin shooting in 1908.

CAN'T TELL THE POLITICIANS WITHOUT A SCORECARD

Harry "Prince Hal" Varnell, a local gambler, became warden of the Cook County Insane Asylum in 1880. He made it *the* place to visit, spending lavishly on fixing up the asylum, throwing parties and even opening the joint to local politicians who needed a friendly place to live. He served one year in the Illinois State Penitentiary, Joliet, for misuse of public funds.

Although there are several accounts of what Varnell did as warden of the insane asylum, we know almost nothing of what became of the inmates. Or if the live-in politicians could be distinguished from the inmates.

Tales of the Lone Star Saloon
and Palm Garden

The inventor of the "Mickey Finn," appropriately named Mickey Finn, was not a very nice person. In fact, he was one of the meanest people in Chicago history.

He owned the Lone Star Saloon and Palm Garden (the "garden" was a back room with a sick potted palm) on South State St., where he sold both the Mickey Finn Special and the Number Two. The Special was raw alcohol, water in which snuff had been soaked and a few drops from Finn's brown bottle filled with unidentified "white stuff." Finn bought that bottle from a voodoo doctor named Hal and it was probably chloral hydrate. Number Two was the same potion, except with beer, instead of alcohol, as the base.

One drink from either potion would knock out the imbiber, after which Finn and his buxom wife, Kate, would drag the customer into a rear "operating room." There, after Finn put on his ritual derby and white apron, the customer would be stripped, robbed, dressed in rags, and tossed into a nearby alley.

Of course, Finn did not become the inventor and distributor of the Mickey Finn without a long apprenticeship. He robbed drunks in Dead Man's Alley, the Bad Lands, Little Cheyenne and Hell's Half-Acre (all Chicago neighborhoods of far-too-colorful repute) during the World's Fair of 1893. He later became a bouncer at Toronto Jim's saloon, but he was fired after he gouged out the eye of a customer with a corkscrew.

Certain rules of decorum were enforced in even the lowest dives of Chicago.

After branching out into pickpocketing, burglary and fencing stolen merchandise, Finn was able to afford to buy the Lone Star. His saloon allowed Finn to live life the way he thought it ought to be lived.

There was a school for pickpockets in the back room and beds for streetwalkers in the basement. Finn also continued his avocation as a fence.

The Lone Star continued to be the most wicked, meanest, lowest dive in Chicago until 1903, when Gold-Tooth Mary offered to buy the place. The negotiations did not proceed according to Robert's Rules of Order, and Gold Tooth Mary eventually stabbed Mickey Finn in the hand with a hat pin. But that didn't bring her any closer to making a deal with Finn.

On Dec. 15, she complained to a City Council committee, saying, "The brutality there is awful, especially since he started serving those horrible drinks." Gold Tooth Mary said that Billy Miller was drugged and robbed of a gold watch and $35, but he complained about the service at the Lone Star. In fact, he wanted his money back. Miller was later found near the railroad tracks with his head cut off.

The Lone Star was closed the next day. Finn sold his Special to other bar owners for several years and today the words "Mickey Finn" apply to knockout drops used anywhere.

Finn never intended to expand the English language. All he wanted to do was to discover a more efficient method for robbing folks—a Chicago entrepreneur.

YOU'D NEED A JAPANESE INFANTRY REGIMENT TO RAID THE PLACE

To set the record straight, once and for all, according to Big Jim O'Leary, neither his mother, Catherine, nor anyone in his immediate family nor their cow ever started the Great Chicago Fire of 1871. Just who set it is still a mystery, although Jim thought it was drunken teenagers, sneaking some milk for a boozy concoction, who upset a lantern, burned down half the town and blamed Mrs. O'Leary for the tragedy.

He was only two years old at the time of the fire. The remaining years allowed Big Jim O'Leary to do a lot more than merely burn down the town.

He became a big-time gambler, a corruptor and perhaps one of the original founders of the infamous Chicago crime syndicate.

During over 40 years as the most visible gambler in Chicago, O'Leary was only caught and convicted once. His fine: $100.

His first big break was the fight between James J. Corbett and John L. Sullivan in 1892. Smart money was on Sullivan, but O'Leary took the four-to-one odds against Corbett and made a fortune when Corbett won in the 21st round.

O'Leary was part of a syndicate which operated the steamboat *City of Traverse* from 1904 to 1907. It was the first gambling ship in American history according to one historian, although that sounds far fetched. Surely someone came up with that idea before 1904. Anyway, police stopped the scheme by arresting the gamblers as they left the ship after it docked.

O'Leary was also involved in an attempt to export Chicago gambling to nearby DuPage County. He built a horse-racing handbook joint there in 1904, and what an odd and forbidding place it was. It had a fence anchored by lookout towers behind which was another fence, this one 14 feet tall with spikes atop it. Vicious dogs patrolled the area between the two fences.

Somehow, the County of DuPage didn't notice the structure, or the thousands of bettors arriving daily on special Santa Fe trains, or the Western Union lines entering the building with reports from five tracks.

But a Chicago newspaper got upset about the building and the $5,000 in weekly bribes allegedly offered to local officials by O'Leary. A local sheriff, after surveying the gambling stockade, said that it would be difficult for "a regiment of Japanese infantry with siege guns" to storm the place. But it was closed anyway, after pressure was put on the railroad and the telegraph company. Soon rail service ceased, the telegraph lines were cut and the entire project faded from memory.

O'Leary was not one to let failure daunt him. His two story "palace of vice" on Chicago's South Side operated with impunity for decades. It was, by all descriptions, the gambling den to end all gambling dens.

He said the place was "fireproof, lightning-proof, bombproof, burglar proof and policeproof." It sure seemed that way. It was bombed three times between 1907 and 1909, with little or no damage. It was raided, but police only found an elderly gentleman reading a prayer book at a kitchen table where a legendary pool hall had once been. Another raid had unfortunate results for the police. O'Leary supposedly put red pepper on his walls. When the police axes struck the walls, the pepper (or maybe zinc) blinded most of the cops and caused three of them to take a week off.

O'Leary's pool hall had beautiful chairs and couches, servants more than willing to bring a tired cushion hitter a fresh drink, and charts with race results. His establishment also boasted a fake chimney with a ladder inside leading to a basement for escape. There was a trap door on the third floor with a ladder which could be pulled up after the escaping gamblers. Another trap door on the third floor was perforated so pepper could be thrown through it at pursuing lawmen.

The oddest thing about the building was that it didn't exist where it was supposed to. O'Leary's on Halsted St. was actually a saloon, with Turkish baths, bowling lanes and the pool hall—all legal enterprises, meaning that any raider would have to separate the illegal gamblers from the legal patrons. The gambling was conducted behind double iron doors which led to an allegedly vacant building next door. Just outside the legal establishment, a fat man with a megaphone was assigned to constantly chant, "Concert inside: All free, all free."

O'Leary boasted, "I've been raided a thousand times, but I've never had a real raid," meaning that his payoffs to police worked for him.

He wasn't even the victim of an actual raid in 1910,

when O'Leary's son, Jim Jr., eloped with the daughter of Inspector William Clancy. Both fathers-in-law were enraged at the match. Imagine the gambler's son marrying the lawman's daughter. The differences between the Montagues and the Capulets are trivial in comparison, but the inspector never led a door-breaking raid on O'Leary's place.

While he lived, O'Leary had a reputation of being willing to bet on anything to maintain his self-proclaimed reputation as "Chicago's real and only king gambler." He claimed to have won $439,690 betting on The Picket in the 1903 American Derby in Washington Park, leading one local sports writer to say it was the biggest horse bet in history. He also claimed to have won $10,000 betting that it would rain 18 days in May of 1908. He claimed he won $1,000 betting it would rain 20 days in April of 1922. Reporters later learned it only rained 19 days that month, but O'Leary answered that the weather records merely noted moisture over the downtown area, while his bet concerned rain over his South Side gambling place.

He got a bit of religion as he aged and one day O'Leary donated a new altar railing for his church. It was said that, after looking at the railing, Big Jim said, "Doesn't that beat hell?" And the priest answered, "That is the point."

When liquor was found in his gambling establishment, O'Leary told the judge that it was left there by a mysterious stranger, who actually bought milk from O'Leary (who claimed that was all he sold that was drinkable), emptied the milk bottles and then poured a mysterious liquor into the bottles. The stranger left before O'Leary could return his milk bottles to him. O'Leary testified that just as O'Leary "ran out to get him . . . the agents pinched the place."

It may be that O'Leary's place was temporarily shut at that time because U.S. District Judge Kenesaw Mountain Landis thought that was the worst lie ever told in a federal court.

When O'Leary died on Jan. 22, 1925, some said he was a millionaire. But Richard T. Griffin, writing in the Chicago Historical Society magazine, said his estate was actually worth only $10,000.

O'Leary bet on everything—football, baseball, boxing, elections, crops and the weather—but he didn't win every time.

CHICAGO'S BEAST AND THE BEAUTY

It may be that, with the assassination of Big Jim Colosimo, we have the first case on record of a pimp being murdered because he loved opera too dearly.

Colosimo began life as a street sweeper, his only honest employment. He married a brothel owner, Victoria Moresco, in 1902; became a Democratic precinct captain of the notorious Levee, meaning he was immune from arrest; ran several whore houses; was a white slaver who supplied women to other brothel owners; and eventually came to control much of Chicago's vice, booze and gambling. During his time at the top, his personal earnings averaged $50,000 a month for eight years. That is a tidy sum now. It was a fortune around 1900.

He was not a shy, unassuming hoodlum. He owned the biggest cars in town, had uniformed servants, wore a diamond ring on every finger, diamond studs in his shirts, diamond cufflinks, had diamonds in his belt and suspender buckles, carried diamonds in bags and often toyed with them.

His proudest possession was Colosimo's Cafe, at 2121 S. Wabash. It became the place to go if you wanted to do a little slumming in Chicago. Because Colosimo was an opera patron, on any given night you might see Galli-Curci, Mary Garden, Tetrazzini or Caruso there. George M. Cohan was often a patron, as were Al Jolson, Sophie Tucker, Ethel and Jack Barrymore, Harold McCormick and Ganna Walska, Sam Insull, and so forth.

They said that Colisimo's lasagna was an "epicure's dream." His chef, Antonio Caesarino, made risotto aux truffes with imported Italian tomatoes.

That was the public Colosimo. The private Colosimo owned four whore houses, earned $10 a trick from other women, needed Johnny Torrio as his body guard because of extortion threats from the Black Hand organization, and was reputed to have killed at least three men attempting to take his money.

He was a beast. He needed his beauty, and he found her.

Dale Winter has been described thus: "She has more than beauty; there is intelligence in her level brown eyes, intelligence and candor and something flamingly clean. It is this clean spirit of Dale Winter's in her free, square gaze that attracts you more than does her lovely voice . . . "

Colosimo met her, fell in love with her, and hired her to sing in his cafe. His wife, Victoria, gave him a divorce without a protest, although there were those who suspected she was really a woman scorned and might have plotted his murder.

Dale and Big Jim were married, but their wedded bliss lasted only three weeks. They spent a lot of time planning Dale Winter's operatic career, with Jim saying, "You don't have to earn a living now. You can rest and study and rest and sing and rest and perform roles in the Auditorium."

That wasn't to be. On May 11, 1920, Colosimo went to his cafe to check on two truckloads of whiskey to be delivered there. A man between 25 and 30 years old, five feet six inches tall, fat faced, dark complexioned, wearing a black derby hat, a black overcoat, patent leather shoes and a white standup collar stepped behind Colosimo as Big Jim stood in front of his cafe. Two shots were fired and one bullet entered behind Colosimo's right ear. He died immediately.

They said that the murder cost $150,000, of which $20,000 went to the gunman and the rest to the Black Hand. Some 150 $1,000 bills in a tin box in Colosimo's safe disappeared the day of the murder.

It was said that Johnny Torrio had imported Frankie Yale, a New York gunman, to murder Colosimo because Torrio thought Big Jim was going soft. After all, Colosimo was now devoted to Dale and she certainly wasn't the professional brothel owner Victoria was.

Although Colosimo was said to be wealthy, his estate was probated at $67,500. Dale Winter said she didn't want a cent of his money, adding, "I am going out of here with the same little suitcase I brought in and that's all I'll take." She later married a theatrical producer and found happiness.

According to some local newsmen, Al Capone, who became Torrio's bodyguard, boasted, "I wiped out Colosimo. He was in love and gettin' soft. I figured it was time he got out and I stepped in. He could have all the women he wanted. When he divorced Victoria, he violated the code of the Mafia. Victoria got her vengeance and I got Chicago."

All of which sums up events rather neatly, except no one is sure Capone really said that and, even if he did, that neglects the successful rule of Torrio.

Colosimo had a huge funeral with 5,000 mourners, including three judges, an Assistant State's Attorney, nine aldermen, plus two Congressmen, a state representative and assorted hoodlums in attendance.

In exchange for three weeks' marriage with a beautiful singer, Jim Colosimo lost his empire, his first wife and his life. One only hopes that Dale sang well.

HE KNEW WHEN TO LEAVE TOWN

In retrospect, Johnny Torrio may have been Chicago's smartest gangster. He escaped with his hide more or less intact after life at the top.

He was undisputed ruler of the underworld for four years, eight months and 13 days, the time between Big Jim Colosimo's murder on May 11, 1920 and the assassination attempt against Torrio on Jan. 24, 1924.

During that time, with a combination of muscle, guile and diplomacy, plus an ability to bribe almost everyone, with a willingness to accept money evidenced by the Big Bill Thompson City Hall, Torrio was able to gross an estimated $70 million a year. That included $5,000 a week net earnings from the Stockade, a whore house in Stickney, Ill.; $200,000 a week from gambling; $3,000,000 a year from whiskey, beer and wine, and so on. He commanded between 700 and 800 gunmen, plus one imported saloon manager and chief gunman named Al Capone. The man imported to protect Colosimo (Torrio) would himself be supplanted by the man he imported to protect him.

It was said that Torrio offered a Chicago police chief $1,000 a day and finally $100,000 a month if Torrio could operate free of police interference. Bribes of $250,000 and $50,000 were sometimes routinely reported by local prosecutors and federal officials.

By all accounts, Torrio's reign worked rather well. The populace had its thirst for illegal alcohol and shady ladies satisfied, the gangsters got more money than they ever dreamed of, and many local law enforcement officials were able to retire in comparative wealth for just looking the other way.

There were problems. Spike O'Donnell tried to run beer into the South Side without the friendly cooperation of Torrio. The result: The first time anyone was "taken for a ride," meaning being driven to a secluded Forest Preserve to be shot and dumped. That happened to George Bucher and George Meeghan, two O'Donnell henchmen. O'Donnell stopped bringing his beer into town when the score got too lopsided: Seven to two, meaning seven of his gunmen died vs. two of Torrio's.

On Jan. 24, 1925, just days before Torrio was to begin serving a nine-month sentence for being in the Sieben Brewery when 13 trucks of illegal brew were being loaded for hijacking, three unknown assassins put bullets into Torrio's jaw, chest, right arm and groin. The pistol's chambers were empty when the gunman attempted to fire the coup de grace, thus saving Torrio's life. It was whispered that the gunmen were Bugs Moran, Hymie Weiss and Vince Drucci.

At that point, Torrio relinquished the leadership of the Chicago underworld to Al Capone. Torrio returned to New York, where perhaps underworld life was a little more peaceful than in Chicago.

The Man Who Liked to Stay Home Nights

Dion O'Banion was an ex-altar boy who loved flowers and his mother. But he had a few character flaws. Among them was the reputation for murdering as few as 25 or as many as 62 people.

The man whose death started Chicago's bloody gangland wars of the '20s was a living contradiction. They said that if he pulled a gun on the wrong party, he'd send a bouquet of flowers as an apology.

He was a theater-goer and first nighter. That interfered with his profession one evening when he shot two brothers in the lobby of the LaSalle Theater. Chicago almost forgave him for that one. One critic, Ashton Stevens, who saw the play and disliked it, wrote, "They shot the wrong men at the theater last night."

O'Banion began not as a gangster but as a newspaper boy, and he later graduated to slugging people to benefit the circulations of the Chicago Tribune and the Herald-American, the Hearst paper. He carried a press card for much of his life as a result of that service. Once, when surrounded by police while he was attempting to blow a safe, it was alleged that he posed as a reporter, flashed his trusty press card, said he was there covering the story, and got away.

They said he never drank beer or whiskey, yet he was a bootlegger. One psychologist said he suffered from "sunny brutality." Others noted that he usually carried three pistols, one in a makeshift codpiece, making him Chicago's only ambidextrous, three-gun hood.

Despite his teetotalling ways, he is supposed to have robbed the Sibley warehouse of 1,750 barrels (!) of bonded whiskey in 1924, substituting water for $1,000,000 worth of the good stuff. He was indicted—but not convicted—for that caper, which stands as one of the biggest heists of all time.

According to George Murray's book, *The Legacy of Al Capone*, O'Banion graduated from the newspaper wars to become a safe-cracker. His sometime partner was Charles "The Ox" Reiser, whose nickname stemmed from the fact that he could lift a safe and move it from one end of an office to another.

This team, plus assistants, is supposed to have blown safes containing $2,000; $2,060; $1,400; $3,865; and $594.61 during 1918, when they worked only four months. The robberies were reported to the police by John Mahoney, who said he worked with O'Banion before branching out on his own. He may be difficult to believe because he was not the smartest person Chicago gangdom ever produced. He was caught attempting to rob the West Side Masonic Temple for the ninth time. One would think that after seven or eight safe-crackings in the same place a guy would move on to something else.

O'Banion also entered the annals of crime when he meekly gave himself up. On June 1, 1921, he attempted to open the safe in the Chicago Typographical Union offices. He was surprised by a policeman and a watchman. O'Banion had a cocked revolver in his hands when the two men came upon him, but he slowly let the hammer down and meekly said, "Don't shoot, we give up." Tough-guy O'Banion later explained that self-preservation and civic pride caused him to do that. The Ox had a pint of nitro in his pocket and, O'Banion said, "One shot in that room would have blown the whole south end of the Loop to Kingdom Come."

When he went to trial for that stunt, he explained that he was having "hot chocolate and chocolate eclairs" at a nearby restaurant at 3 a.m. when he heard a noise. He climbed a fire escape and the noise of his arrival must have frightened away the true safe crackers. When the police arrived, O'Banion claimed he thought they were the crooks, so he drew his pistol. He added, "But when I saw it was a policeman, I put my gun down and we gave ourselves up like good citizens." The jury believed him, although the jurors may have taken into account his fellow defendant, the Ox, who tended to murder witnesses, jurors and everyone else who accused him of wrong-doing. O'Banion was found not guilty.

Meanwhile, O'Banion branched out into bootlegging. He controlled the North Side's liquor supply during Prohibition, delivering his fire water in trucks from his flower shop. Eventually, as many gangsters did, he dabbled in politics with methods which assured the desired results. During the November, 1924, elections, O'Banion decided that his ward should be Republican rather than Democratic.

O'Banion would go to the neighborhood saloons, and would begin shooting. His favorite target was the toilet doorknobs, something which didn't make him overly popular with the beery patrons. But it got his point across and 98 per cent of the ward voted Republican. No one wanted to lose any more doorknobs to such valuable places.

His electioneering efforts were preceded by one of the most amazing dinners in Chicago political history. The Democrats tried to win his support by giving him a testimonial, during which he received a $1,500 platinum watch and applause from the Democratic candidate for U.S. Senator, a police lieutenant, the county clerk and the chief of detectives. It was, by all accounts, a grand evening, which was only marred when Leland Verain alias Louie Alterie alias "Cowboy" or "Two-Gun" pulled a gun on the waiter, but then Louis always had a temper.

So did O'Banion, plus a desire for revenge. After Samuel J. "Nails" Morton, a gang member and a man who could quickly sell a truck-load of stolen whiskey, was kicked to death by a horse, the O'Banion gang kidnapped the horse and "took it for a ride." The horse was taken back to the spot where it kicked Morton and was shot, gangland style. That horse never kicked another gangster again, but we're not sure if other horses learned their lesson as well.

Despite his many crimes and adventures, O'Banion led a quiet home life. His wife claimed he loved to "stay home nights" sitting in his slippers listening to the radio and "singing a song." He once even paid for a crippled kid to go to the Mayo Clinic. His wife added, "Dion was a simple man. He never left home without telling me where he was going. He was seldom out at night. I was his only sweetheart. He hated ostentation. He had one small car, a little sedan he bought for me."

As far as is known, his marriage and his gang life were kept quite separate. They came together forcefully on the day he died.

There are differing theories as to why O'Banion was assassinated and by whom. Herbert Asbury wrote that O'Banion was expanding and Johnny Torrio, then leader of Chicago gangdom, wanted a share of the wealth, which O'Banion refused to give. Asbury also wrote that O'Banion didn't like the Terrible Gennas, the brothers Sam, Jim, Pete, Angelo, Tony and Mike, who

were selling cheaper hootch to the same customers that
O'Banion was. O'Banion was supposed to have hijacked
a Genna truck loaded with $30,000 worth of whiskey,
something no one in their right mind would do, and
then refused to forgive a Genna gambling debt.
O'Banion, professing to be afraid of the Gennas, even
offered to sell his brewery and retire. After Torrio and
Al Capone bought the place for a reported $500,000, it
was raided and Torrio plus 27 others (including
O'Banion) were arrested. Furthermore, all the beer in
the place, 13 trucks of the stuff, was confiscated by the
authorities, who were sent there allegedly by O'Banion.

O'Banion is supposed to have rejected peace over-
tures between himself and the "Terrible" Gennas by
saying, "oh, to hell with them Sicilians" (Asbury) or by
referring to them as a "bunch of spic pimps" (George
Murray).

In any case, Mike Merlo, president of the Unione
Siciliane (Mafia) and peacemaker for a generation of
hoods, died just five days after the election of 1924.
Two days later, at about noon, Nov. 10, O'Banion was
preparing floral displays for Merlo's funeral when three
men entered his shop. O'Banion said, "Hello, boys, you
want Merlo's flowers?"

Then, according to two out of three historians, Albert
Anselmi, John Scalisi and Mike Genna began shooting
at the florist-bootlegger. (One historian, George
Murray, wrote that it was James Genna, Pete Gusenberg
and Carmen Vacco, and the coroner thought it was
Scalisi, Anselmi and dependable Frankie Yale who shot
O'Banion.) Anselmi and Scalisi, who supposedly fired

some of the guns used in the St. Valentine's Day Massacre, got $10,000 and a diamond ring for dispatching O'Banion. Both were later personally beaten to death by Al Capone (it was rumored), who used a baseball bat on their persons, breaking nearly every bone in their bodies. Their profession was not appreciated.

Someone, probably the Genna in the bunch, was shaking O'Banion's hand (his left hand held pruning shears) when six shots entered his head, chest, cheek and larynx, "all in one lightning-fast volley that sent him crashing back dead into a showcase full of crysanthemums and roses," according to the Daily News.

William Crutchfield, the porter on the scene, said he saw two Italians and a Greek or a Jew enter the shop. After that, he wisely saw nothing, heard nothing and said nothing.

O'Banion was laid to rest in style, reposing within a $10,000 silver-bronze coffin, with silver angels standing at the head and foot of the casket and a slab on the coffin saying, "Suffer the little children to come unto me." Some 40,000 people saw the body and two dozen trucks and cars were needed to carry all the flowers to the gravesite.

But death did not stop O'Banion from affecting the lives of others.

Father Patrick Malloy, O'Banion's boyhood buddy, conducted services in the funeral home and at graveside, despite the fact that the Cardinal decreed that no requiem mass or extreme unction be given to O'Banion. Father Malloy's disobedience was not forgotten.

Six years later, when John "Dingbat" Oberta, a Polish hood who like to put an apostrophe (O'Berta") in his name and speak in a brogue to Irishmen, was shot during a battle over control of a union, Father Malloy allegedly again said a few words at the wake and at graveside.

According to George Murray's *The Legacy of Al Capone*, for those two transgressions of a Cardinal's order, Father Malloy was banished from Chicago for six years.

Now Father Malloy was a rather special priest. It was said that one night this "Friend of the Friendless" arrived at his parish house at 3 a.m. and saw a brawny man tearing up his newly sodded lawn, preparing to steal it by putting it in a nearby truck. Father Malloy drew his revolver, held it against the man's neck and ordered him to put the sod back. The man, upon whirling around and seeing a pistol-packing priest, fainted. Father Malloy revived him by sprinkling some non-holy water from a garden hose. This time the pistol was pointed between the man's eyes. He got the idea and put the sod back, after which, according to Murray's book, Father Malloy gave him his blessing and put his pistol away.

After the O'Banion and Oberta funerals, Father Malloy's exile was swift and absolute. He was put on a train for New York and placed on a boat bound for Buenos Aires, where he was given no duties whatsoever. He learned how to make poison darts and how to shoot them from a blowgun (the next sod rustler had better beware!) and he collected walking sticks until friends interceded with the Cardinal, who allowed him back to Chicago in 1942. But then the Catholic Church of Chicago has never been a pushover. Six years in the Amazon jungles for two funeral services stood as testimony to Father Malloy's loyalty to his friends.

THE DEATH OF HOP TOAD AND OTHERS

Folks around Chicago still sometimes speak reverently about Al Capone because of his soup kitchens, which fed thousands during the Depression. He is also known for allegedly beating in the heads of three of his torpedoes during a dinner, of kicking and beating his hand-picked Mayor of Cicero in front of Cicero's police force which was afraid to save the guy, and of bringing Chicago unwanted fame through his uncounted murders. He died after his syphilis drove him insane, meaning that some of the retribution for his sins was visited upon him during his stay on this earth.

On May 8, 1929, the bodies of Joseph Giunta, called "Hop Toad" because of his madness for jazz dancing; John Scalise and Albert Anselmi were found in Hammond, Ind., their heads—and most of their bodies—bashed in with a sawed-off baseball bat. It was whispered that the murders were Al Capone's after-dinner entertainment—his revenge for their plots against his life.

He was called "Scarface" because of a scar on his left cheek. He sometimes said the scars were war wounds, but knowledgeable folks claimed he got the scars during a fight in a Brooklyn dance hall.

During his rule of the underworld, there were 29 rub-outs in four months of 1926. Between 1927 and 1930, there were 227 gang killings in Chicago. By 1929, it was estimated that his various rackets were costing Chicagoans $136,000,000 a year, or $45 for every man, woman and child in Chicago.

Capone was nearly ultimately inconvenienced on Jan. 12, 1925, and again on Sept. 20, 1926.

In the first instance, while Capone's car was parked in front of a restaurant, it was fired upon with shotguns and machine guns carried by Bugs Moran and others. Capone wasn't in the car at the time.

During the second attack, 10 cars slowly drove past the Hawthorne Inn in Cicero, firing 1,000 rounds in less than 10 seconds. A man in a khaki shirt got out of the sixth car, stood at the door of the restaurant and fired 100 shells from his machine gun. Capone escaped by diving to the floor. He was later reported to have spent $10,000 to save the sight of Mrs. Clyde Freeman, whose right eye was injured by flying glass during the attack.

Shooting incidents like that led Hollywood to become enamored of Capone. He has been portrayed in the movies by Edward G. Robinson ("Little Caesar" and "Key Largo"), Rod Steiger ("Al Capone"), Jason Robards Jr. ("The St. Valentine's Day Massacre," which included the death-by-baseball bat scene), Neville Brand ("The Scarface Mob") and George Raft ("Some Like It Hot").

The St. Valentine's Day Massacre represented both the height of Capone's disregard for human life and the beginning of the end for him.

Just after 10 a.m., Feb. 14, 1929, two "policemen" and two plainclothesmen stepped into a Chicago garage and held members of the Bugs Moran gang at bay. According to most accounts, John Scalise and Joseph Lolordo each began machine gunning from opposite ends of the line-up, killing seven men, including Reinhardt H. Schwimmer, an optometrist who stopped by because he loved to talk to gangsters.

Those murdered included Johnnie May, a safe-cracker; Frank and Pete Gusenberg, gunmen; Adam Heyer, embezzler; Al Weinshank, speakeasy owner; James Clark, Moran's brother-in-law; and Schwimmer.

In reporting the scene, the Daily News wrote:

It's too much to tell. You go into the door marked 'S-M-C Cartage Co.' You see a bunch of big men talking with restrained excitement in the cigarette smoke. You go through another door back of the front office. You go between two close-parked trucks in the garage.

Then you almost stumble over the head of the first man, with a clean gray felt hat still placed at the precise angle of gangster toughness.

The dull yellow of a lamp . . . shows rivulets of blood heading down to the drain that was meant for the water from the washed cars. There are six of the red streams from six heads. The bodies—four of them well dressed in civilian clothes—two of them with their legs crossed as they whirled to fall . . .

The crowd (outside) was a cross section. Gold Coast and Clark Street merged in the gathering.

What is it? Who were they?

Inside, six pairs of lips failed to answer.

A seventh pair of lips, Frank Gusenberg, momentarily survived the carnage. He was asked who shot him and his last words were, "Nobody shot me."

There were those who wished they had shot Frank Gusenberg. The next day, two women, Mrs. Lucille Gusenberg and Mrs. Ruth Gusenberg, went to the Drake-Braithwaite Funeral Home to claim the body of the man each thought was their truly beloved husband. Neither knew of the existence of the other and they had a lot to talk about.

During an interview, Al Capone said, "Only Bugs Moran kills like that." During a separate interview in the hospital room where he was hiding out (Moran was about to enter the garage when he saw the approaching "police" car and so he ducked out of sight), Bugs Moran said, "Only Capone kills like that." History—and the authorities of the day—believed Moran.

People couldn't forget the St. Valentine's Day Massacre. Federal officials became quite interested in Capone, who was finally found guilty of income tax evasion in 1931 and who was sentenced to 10 years in prison. During that trial, one Capone gunman, Philip D'Andrea, was found in court with a .38 calibre revolver, extra ammunition, the star of a deputy bailiff and an identification card from the West Chicago police department.

By the time Capone got out of jail, disease had ravaged his brain. The many people he put in graves would only wish that it had happened earlier.

THE ULTIMATE ANTI-CRIME VEHICLE

Local officials have gone to great lengths in the interest of good law enforcement, but perhaps no one has gone farther than Illinois Governor Dwight Green, who introduced the "perfect" crime fighting machine in 1942.

It cost $80,000 and it could battle the forces of evil anywhere and everywhere. It was a huge, armor-plated bus, with diving equipment, a crime laboratory, dog cages, a photo lab, hospital and arsenal. It had a machine gun turret on top.

The governor thought it would be suitable for riots, disasters, prison breaks and drownings. He even boasted that it could speed to the scene of trouble at 65 miles per hour.

Unfortunately, as journalist Mike Royko later pointed out, it was 8,000 pounds over the legal limit for a vehicle on an Illinois highway. And the moment it left the highway, it sank into the ground.

Illinois got rid of its perfect crime fighting vehicle in 1948 for $3,700.

"I DON'T KNOW NOTHIN' ABOUT NOTHIN'. I CAN PROVE IT."

For a while there, everything not nailed down was liable to be stolen by the energetic Panczkos, brothers in thievery. Hell, they even allegedly stole a two-ton cement mixer in 1957 and tried to sell it for $36.

Joseph "Pops" Panczko, probably the most famous of the three brothers, once asked newsmen to "just call me the Polish Robin Hood." Pops, Butch and Peanuts did seem to enjoy both liberating other people's property and making headlines when getting caught.

Butch once used as his alibi, "I don't know nothin' about nothin'. I can prove it," which would have been a fascinating philosophical exercise.

Pops, who had over 70 arrests on his ledger, was first caught in 1940 while attempting to move a safe out of a drug store.

During one robbery involving Peanuts and four others, $1,750,000 worth of jewelry was stolen. That was the easy part. Getting away was tough.

Four of the gang made it to the getaway car and backed up, almost running over the fifth. By the time the quintet was inside the car, another automobile had pulled up, pinning the getaway vehicle in place for a while.

The gang then raced to the sea, where they had two motorboats waiting. One boat wouldn't start and the five men couldn't fit in the remaining vessel. So a tow-line was rigged to the second boat and the frantic getaway was started once more. Then the towline broke. Less than two hours later, all were captured.

Then after 30 years of hard work, the three Panczkos fell on hard times. Pops got a two-year sentence for putting slugs instead of 40 cents into a pay telephone; Butch allegedly retired; Peanuts got 15 years for counterfeiting and another 15 years for jury tampering; and Peanuts' wife got five years for tampering along with Peanuts.

You know, when you get in your 50s and you are a

veteran of more than 70 arrests, mostly for the art of burglary, it must be the worst ignominy to be jailed for putting 40 cents worth of slugs in a pay phone. Chicago just never learned how to treat its headline hunters with respect.

Chapter Six: The Pioneers

"A church and a WCTU never growed
a big town yet. You got to start
with entertainment."
 Cap Streeter

Chicago's—and America's—pioneers have been smothered in saccharine romance.

According to many contemporary writers, no man or woman who was the first to do anything more than 150 years ago—even if it was as minor as being the first person to slaughter a hog in town—was ever snippy or snappy, was ever corrupt or compelled by less than virtuous motives. They always stood at history's door, shoulders squared, eyes steely, chests expanded, jaws firm and all motives resolved.

In fact, the folks who created America have now become monumental bores, given to Revolutionary War bumper-sticker platitudes.

Chicago's pioneers were a diverse lot—religious fanatics, fast-buck traders, and so on. Nobody really wanted to come to the gooey swamp that was Chicago unless God, conquests or profit motives compelled them.

What would these now-mythical pioneers say if they

told the truth about themselves? Would we recognize or believe the truth if we heard it? Probably not.

What follows are some very different stories about The Pioneers. Too bad we do not know even more such tales—our Pioneering Bores might return to us as humans who often surpassed themselves.

CRACKED CORN MAKERS ???

No one knows what the name "Chicago" means.

It was certainly an Indian word or phrase, but that's about all we know for sure.

It could have come from Chocago, Checagou, Chikilgo, Checaguar, Chicopo, Chictgoo, Che-guag-ga-winshe, Cakorego, Shegagh, Shilgogu, Shegaug, Shih-guag-go, Shikakawanz, Shigacho, Shekgua, Cheagoumeinan or the brain-shattering, mouth-twisting Pakawasigaminikewininug.

Local supporters often denied that Chicago actually meant stink weed and that the entire town was named after wild onion, crow garlic or skunk weed (allium vineale) which grew in the bog which later became Chicago. However, a French explorer, Joutel, said in 1687 that he arrived at a place called "Chicagou," which was named because of the "quantity of garlic growing in this district . . . "

Others say that "Chicago" meant great or strong. However, the Chicago River was neither great nor strong then or now. Today it is only great or strong when it smells, which brings us back to stinking garlic weeds.

To translate a few of the possible Indian names: Shikakawanz means garlic, Shekagu or Chikilgo means skunk, Chi or Gitchi and Kago mean strong thing. Finally the word Pakwasigaminikewininug was Algonquin for "cracked corn makers."

If you want to believe that Chicago meant "Cracked Corn Makers," go ahead, but I think it merely confuses an already murky situation.

What Do You Say to a Naked Old Man?

Chicago was discovered by two men looking for something else—either a water route to the Orient or God.

Fur-trader Louis Jolliet was ordered to travel upon the Mississippi River so he might find "Quivira, which with its gold and precious stones was believed to lie in the path to the California Sea." Father Jacques Marquette was supposed to go along for the ride "to seek new nations toward the South Sea, to teach them of the Great God whom they have hitherto unknown."

Marquette and Jolliet started in May, 1673, in Quebec and were on the Arkansas River by July, with information that the Mississippi ran to the Gulf of Mexico and not to the Pacific. Having determined that they were going in the wrong direction, they turned around, took the Illinois River and eventually went through Chicago, noting that a small canal could connect Lake Michigan and the St. Lawrence to the Gulf of Mexico. It was logical, but the St. Lawrence Seaway would take civilized man three centuries to complete.

During their momentous trek, they frequently met friendly Indians under disquieting circumstances. For instance, according to Marquette's diary, they met "an old man who awaited us with a rather surprising attitude, which constitutes a part of the Ceremonial that they (the Indians) observe when they receive strangers. This man stood erect, and stark naked, his hands extended and lifted toward the sun . . . When we came near him, he paid us This Compliment, "How beautiful the sun is, Oh Frenchman, when thou comest to visit us! All our village awaits thee, and thou shalt enter all our cabins in peace."

The exploring duo seemed to have made it a habit of being greeted by nude old codgers. A few pages later in his journal, Marquette noted, "When we reached the village of the Great Captain, we saw him at the entrance to his Cabin, between two old men—all three erect and naked and holding their Calumet (peace pipe) turned toward the sun . . . He afterward offered us his Calumet, and made us smoke while we entered his Cabin, where we received all their usual kind attentions."

Father Marquette also observed that men of the Illinois tribe cut off the noses and ears of their straying wives, but he made no numerical survey of the percentages of noseless, earless women among the Illinois.

Marquette took sick during a winter near Chicago (as so many have since that time). He died near Ludington, Mich., on May 18, 1675. He was almost 38 years old.

We Can Get It for You
Cheaper Than New York

On Aug. 20, 1794, "Mad Anthony" Wayne led more
than 4,000 infantry and cavalry against 2,000 Indians,
led by Chief Little Turtle.

Capt. William Well, later the hero of the Fort Dearborn Massacre, was a scout for Gen. Wayne. He thus
completed surely one of the most dramatic shifts in
allegiance in American history. Just four years before,
Wells fought beside his "father", Little Turtle, against
St. Clair. Little Turtle had kidnapped Wells when Wells
was a child. On this day in 1794, Wells would battle
Little Turtle. Fathers everywhere should learn something or other from that.

It would be called the Battle of Fallen Timbers
because the Indians chose to fight in a tornado-
wrecked forest, with trees strewn about. They lost,
decisively, and one year later Little Turtle and 93 other
chiefs gave up 25,000 square miles of their territory,
including "one piece of Land Six Miles Square at the
mouth of the Chickago River emptying into the South-
west end of Lake Michigan where a fort formerly
stood."

It was perfectly all right with the Indians to give up
that "Six Miles Square" of land, which later became
downtown Chicago. Little Turtle told Gen. Wayne that
he had never heard of the place.

And that was how the white man got possession of
Chicago. Not for $24, as in the case of Manhattan; no
romance or decisive moment; just "haven't heard of the
place, so take it."

THE FIRST DISAPPOINTED MAN IN CHICAGO

We know very little about Chicago's alleged first settler, Jean Baptiste Point du Sable, a French Canadian who was either a mulatto or a Negro and who may or may not have been the first settler.

There was another man, Pierre Moreau, known as The Mole, who stayed around Chicago for a while about that time. But he was a pioneer bootlegger who has been nearly ignored by the good citizens of Chicago. How would you like your town to be started by a French bootlegger?

There may have been a third man, another trader lurking in the woods, a man by the name of either Guary or Guillory or maybe Guyair, who probably gave his name to the city of Gary, Ind. But he didn't leave much paperwork behind (deeds, marriages, etc.), so he, too, lost the first settler award.

DuSable was another story. There is a 1779 reference to him stating, "Baptiste Point DeSaible, a handsome negro, well educated and settled at Eschikagou; but much in the French interest." Now *that's* more like the image of the proper, heroic pioneer.

It is said that DuSable (or DeSaible) was from Santo Domingo, and that he traded in the Chicago area from 1779 to 1796. He was described as "a large man; that he had a commission for some office, but for what particular office or from what government, I cannot now recollect." Augustin Grignon added, "He was a trader, pretty wealthy and drank freely."

According to Milo M. Quaife's book, *Checagou*, DuSable married a Cahokian Indian woman, Catherine, on Oct. 27, 1788. Just two years later, the DuSable's daughter, Susanne, was married. Life moved swiftly on the frontier.

He also allegedly tried to become head of the Pottawatomie Indians, but failed. He eventually sold his Chicago property for $1,200 including: a French walnut cabinet with four glass doors, four tables, seven chairs, one bureau, a couch, a stove, and one large feather bed, plus mirrors, lanterns, candlesticks, a dairy, a mill, a bakehouse, a poultry house, two barns, a workshop, 44 hens, 28 hogs, 30 cattle, two calves, two mules, eight axes, eight sickles, seven scythes, three carts, a plow and 11 copper kettles.

From that inventory, the man seemed to have done quite well for himself, but historians have written that he left town "the first disappointed man in Chicago" because the Pottawatomies rejected him.

He died, historians have noted, in either 1796 or 1814, having spent some time in a debtors' prison. By the way, history would be a lot easier to believe if a few historians worked as journalists before writing anything down. As far as DuSable was concerned, they didn't know exactly when he was born, when he died or how to spell his name. Other than that, the historians are, well, somewhat certain of their facts.

THE FIRST MAN WITH CLOUT ON THE FRONTIER

John Kinzie was a friend to the Indians when that wasn't very popular. One historian even wrote that this Chicago pioneer had "gone Indian" because he had "lived with them, eaten with them, slept with them and protected them with an intense devotion . . . John Kinzie did little to advance the cause of white man's civilization in the Northwest."

That might have been written because John Kinzie insisted on selling whiskey to the Indians. He didn't do that by the drink. He was dispensing booze in 68-gallon casks.

Any impression of Kinzie is difficult because much of what we know of him was written by his loving daughter-in-law, who was surely not impartial.

He has been called "the real founder of Chicago" and "the father of Chicago," while others saw Kinzie as "holding the Indian as nothing more than a source of profit, who might be soaked in liquor if it suited the purposes of those who dealt with him."

Kinzie, who was born about 1763, became a silversmith and spent a lot of time wandering about, trading with the Indians. His first wife, Margaret McKinzie, was kidnapped by the Shawnees at the age of 10. She spent a decade in captivity, found her way to Detroit, met and married Kinzie, had three children by him. When she again met her father, after a separation of many, many years, she quickly returned to Virginia with papa, taking the children and never setting eyes on John Kinzie again. Her heart belonged to daddy.

Kinzie later married Eleanor Little, the widow of Daniel McKillip, who supported the British, who fought beside the Indians and who died with them during the Battle of Fallen Timbers. Eleanor's father also favored the British during the Revolution, and narrowly escaped lynching in Pittsburgh in 1783 because of his beliefs.

The family had problems even before that, according to Milo Quaife. Indians raided the family home in 1779, kidnapping Eleanor, her mother and sister. One wonders what were the odds against a man, Kinzie, marrying two women, both of whom had been kidnapped by Indians before puberty. Either Kinzie was attracted to formerly kidnapped women or the Indians were nabbing every other woman on the frontier.

Kinzie had four children with Eleanor and bought out the Indian trading business of Jean LaLime in 1804. LaLime, who bought his home from DuSable (or DeSaible), remained in Chicago, acting as interpreter between the Indians and the fort and causing trouble for Kinzie.

Fort Dearborn was small and precariously situated in the midst of possibly hostile Indians, but that didn't prevent the doughty pioneers from constant bickering and backstabbing. Kinzie's partnership with the commandant's older son, John Whistler Jr., ended with a dispute which got so heated that folks in Detroit heard about it. To calm things, Capt. John Whistler Sr. was recalled, as were all of Fort Dearborn's officers, who were assigned to various outposts throughout the frontier. That action, which meant that Detroit sided with Kinzie, led many historians to conclude that John Kinzie was the first man with clout on the old frontier.

However, that didn't get rid of LaLime. Both Kinzie and LaLime had nasty tempers. One spring day, as both were leaving the fort, the officer of the day, a Lt. Helm, shouted at Kinzie to watch out because LaLime was close behind him.

There was a fight, during which LaLime shot Kinzie in the shoulder (or possibly the neck—accounts vary). LaLime then drew his "dirk" and the struggle continued, until LaLime was killed. Some said Kinzie murdered LaLime, but pioneer murderers don't get contemporary streets named after them, so let's forget that accusation.

Kinzie fled to Milwaukee and hid there until the officers of the fort, who were LaLime's friends, offered the surprising ruling that the killing was "justifiable homicide." Kinzie returned to Chicago, only to find that other officers had buried LaLime in Kinzie's front yard. Instead of being upset, Kinzie put a fence around the grave and tended it for the rest of his life, the first successful public relations gesture in Chicago's history.

With Kinzie's death, LaLime's bones were forgotten, only to be accidentally dug up when a foundation for another structure was being created. The bones were put in a soapbox and were eventually given to the Chicago Historical Society, which put them in a glass case. No one is sure if LaLime would have wanted that.

Kinzie's friendliness with the Indians paid off during the Fort Dearborn massacre (see chapter seven: Indians) because his home and property were protected throughout the bloody incident. By the way, his family was also saved. But the Massacre didn't prevent Kinzie from being inconvenienced.

Kinzie, his wife, four children and a clerk named John Baptiste Chandonnait (or Chandonnais or Chandonet—no one knows for sure because few people could spell on the frontier) eventually made it to Detroit, where they became prisoners of war of the British. Kinzie was later taken to Fort Malden on suspicion of communicating with the Americans; then to Quebec, where he was loaded on a boat bound for England. The British were going to make darned sure Kinzie didn't communicate with Americans.

But the boat met an American frigate and fled to Halifax. The ship sprung a leak during a second try at reaching England and had to return to port. With two failures at giving Kinzie a free trip to England, the British called it quits. Kinzie was reunited with his family at the end of the war of 1812.

After Kinzie's death, the Pottawatomies signed a treaty which provided his wife and children with $3,500 "in consideration of the attachment of the Indians to her deceased husband, who was long an Indian trader, and who lost a large sum in the trade by the credits given them . . . "

John Kinzie was a tough guy pioneer who knew that sometimes a man's heart, soul and pocketbook could be made a lot easier with 68 gallons of good booze.

THE ACTUAL FATHERS OF CHICAGO

When we think of "pioneers," we think of stoical men in coonskin caps with Bowie knives, hacking their way through a forest, trailed by brave wives dressed in gingham and able to shoot an Indian in the eye at 200 yards. Jean Baptiste and "Jolly Mark" Beaubein were two early Chicagoans who went out of their way to destroy that image.

Jean Baptiste was the first colonel of the Cook County militia, but he was also known for populating much of the town. He fathered 20 children. At the age of 68, he married for the third time and proceeded to have four more children before his death at age 75—possibly due to terminal tiredness.

"Jolly Mark" fathered 23 children and was a fiddle-playing inn keeper. He owned the Sauganash Hotel, described in 1833 as a "vile two-story barrack" which was "dirty in the extreme and confusion reigned throughout." One reason it was "vile" was that Beaubein didn't really run it. He spent most of his time racing horses, shooting ducks from his front porch and fiddling.

Within the Sauganash Hotel, which was really a two-story addition to Mark Beaubein's one-room log shack and for which the rent could go as high as $5 a week, the owner never, ever ran out of beds. Mark Beaubein had discovered an instant method of expansion which was incredibly successful and which, as far as can be determined, no other hotel owner in history has copied.

When the Sauganash got crowded, Beaubein would rent a blanket to a recent arrival and would allow his new guest to cover himself while sleeping on the floor. But the guest would be warned, "Look out, because the Indians may steal it."

"Then," Jolly Mark Beaubein once boasted, "when he gets to sleep, I take the blanket away carefully and give it to another man and tell him the same, so I always have beds for all that want them."

Let's Incorporate without Russell E. Heacock

The incorporation of a city should be accompanied with pomp and ceremony suitable for a heroic tableau or frieze, at the very least. Chicago's incorporation was accompanied by mystery, skullduggery and perhaps a bit of crookedness.

No one knows how many people were actually in Chicago when it was incorporated on Aug. 10, 1833. One historian claimed there were 250 inhabitants with six lawyers, eight doctors (if we can believe there was one doctor for every 31 residents!) and only four taverns (*Epic of Chicago*, by Henry Raymond Hamilton). Another writer thought there were "less than" 1,000 folks here and they had two public buildings—a jail and a hog pound (*The World's Fair City*, 1892).

A preliminary election was held on Aug. 5 and only 13 voters showed up. Only Russell E. Heacock voted against incorporating, but he lived outside the proposed city limits and no one knew how he snuck in to vote anyway.

The voters were invited to Mark Beaubein's home on Aug. 10 and 28 showed up. Of those, 13 became candidates for office.

Chicago needed 150 inhabitants to incorporate. The rule of thumb of the day was that each voter represented five other non-voting souls, meaning that Chicago had 140 residents at most.

Folks just passing through (there were no tourists in those days) were counted and the village was allowed to incorporate.

THE MIDNIGHT RIDE OF GURDON S. HUBBARD

Hubbard St. in Chicago is a mean little thoroughfare, petering out at a nearly subterranean Wacker Dr. and continuing past some quickly fading ancient buildings.

Perhaps it is because of the mean nature of the street that almost no one remembers or honors Gurdon S. Hubbard, a true pioneer, a genuine hero and a great businessman. Chicago has never treated its pioneers with the respect due them.

After reading about all of the innovations and firsts credited to him, one gets the distinct impression that without Gurdon Staltonstall Hubbard, Chicago just wouldn't have been.

Hubbard first arrived in Chicago in 1818. He was a 16-year-old fur trader for John Jacob Astor's American Fur Company, which was doing battle for the Northwest with the British Hudson Bay Co. Hubbard stayed in Chicago for three days and wept as he left because the people there reminded him of home.

In subsequent years, Hubbard returned to start Chicago's first packing business (he slaughtered hogs and piled their carcasses on the river front to freeze during the winter of 1828-29), built the city's first brick building (immediately dubbed "Hubbard's Folly"), became the city's first insurance underwriter, bought the first fire engine, was the first banker, was an early Republican and a supporter of Abraham Lincoln, and lived to see the fire of 1871.

History mainly gossips about three events in his life: His relationship with an Indian lass, his actions during the Winnebago Panic and his business acumen.

Historians often note that Hubbard "cast aside" his Pottawatomie wife, Watseka, and their two half-breed children. Obviously, in those days, one could "cast aside" without the interference of judges, lawyers, courts or therapists.

Hubbard said, "It's true that our relationship started out, like most of those trader-Indian marriage alliances, as a sort of commercial treaty, but I guess we really fell in love after a bit. We were faithful to each other."

The Indians were heading West, Hubbard was getting out of the fur trade (he had been saying, "No more Indians, no more furs"), and the "marriage arrived at a crossroads." Either Watseka would become a "white squaw" and stay with Hubbard, or Hubbard would have to turn Indian and leave with her. They decided to part, but there was much pain to the decision and no mere "casting aside." So let us hear no more criticism of either Hubbard or Watseka on that score.

Hubbard, who originally created a trail which later became State Street, was also known as Pa-ea-ma-ta-be or "Swift Walker" because he could out-walk, out-run any person, Indian or white, on the frontier. And that came in handy during the Winnebago Scare.

It was reported during July of 1827 that the Winnebagos were on the warpath. Chicago thought it needed help, especially since a local chief, named Big Foot, was in cahoots with the Winnebagos. The 40 or so settlers around Fort Dearborn were panic-stricken, even though the nearest Winnebago villages were 200 miles away in Wisconsin.

Hubbard then volunteered to ride 125 miles to

Danville to get help. The world has long since forgotten the 125-mile dash of Gurdon Staltonstall Hubbard. No songs have been written about his bravery, no poems about his mighty deed.

He left on horseback around 4 p.m. It had rained that season and the 125 miles was a flood plain, with rivers overflowing their banks and streams becoming raging torrents. Hubbard changed horses at the Iroquois River, but couldn't get his horse to cross Sugar Creek at night. By morning he discovered that a large tree had fallen in the water, making passage impossible. But Hubbard swam the creek and arrived in Danville at noon, going 125 miles in less than 20 hours, travelling most of the time in darkness, over land without roads or bridges, across rivers and streams which were impassable. One historian has written that, in comparison with Hubbard's feat, "the midnight ride of Paul Revere was mere child's play."

In Danville, 100 men volunteered to save Chicago. They were armed with squirrel rifles, flint locks, muskets, tomahawks and axes, and carried five days' rations.

The group arrived at the swollen Vermillion River on the way to Chicago, but couldn't cross it. Then Hubbard threw off his coat and shouted, "Give me Old Charley."

Hubbard mounted this trusty steed and rode him into the stream, with the other horses coming after him. In mid-stream, Old Charley decided he was in over his head and became unmanageable. Hubbard dismounted, grabbed Old Charley's mane and swam ahead of the animal, using only his left arm to plough through the raging river. The volunteers held their breath, fearful that Hubbard would be washed under the horse or the horse would kick him. But he made it to the other side and eventually so did the other volunteers.

Alas, all that bravery went for naught (which might be why Hubbard's ride is not remembered in story, song, epic, etc.) The volunteers arrived at Fort Dearborn and immediately caused problems. The inhabitants of Chicago were jealous because the volunteers looked better than the Americans, Canadians, half-breeds and "idle, vagabond Indians loitering about," who made up Chicago's population at the time.

Then, after guarding the Fort day and night for 10 days, a runner arrived to announce that the Winnebagos had signed a treaty and the frontier was peaceful once more.

The people of Chicago were overjoyed at the news. To make sure that the trip from Danville wasn't a total loss, there was a party. One barrel each of gin, brandy and whiskey was opened, and everyone had a good time. But it was a hell of a long way to go for a party.

The third characteristic for which Hubbard is famous is even closer to the heart of Chicago than his relationship with Indian wenches or his bravery in traveling to Danville (an act which requires a certain level of folly even today).

Gurdon Hubbard, who began his professional life bound for seven years to work for the American Fur Company at $120 a year, was an incredible buyer of real estate. He bought two Chicago lots, 80 by 100 feet in

size, for $33.33 each in 1829. Six years later, during a
land boom, he sold the lots for an $80,000 profit. In
1835, he bought 80 acres of the most undesirable
Chicago land for $5,000. Hubbard visited New York
and sold the 80 acres for $80,000, realizing a $75,000
profit in 90 days.

Gurdon Hubbard—first with the Indians, first to
Danville and one of the first to make a fortune off of
New York sharpies.

He Fought the Entire Chicago Police Force to a Draw for Three Decades

After one gun battle during Cap Streeter's 30 Years' War
with the Chicago police and the City Establisment, Cap
was arrested, but was quickly released. It seems that,
back in the 1890s, there was no law on the books against
shooting at—but not wounding—a Chicago police
officer.

Cap Streeter may have been Chicago's last pioneer,
although some say that title should go to Hugh
"Playboy" Hefner. During his time in the city, Cap
defied the laws of Illinois and Chicago, fought the
courts and the police to a standstill, hired his own police
force (which eventually struck for higher pay) and
happily kept the town either in wild amusement or
glowering anger for three decades.

By the time Cap arrived in Chicago, he had roamed
the West, served in the Civil War battles of Missionary
Ridge and Lookout Mountain, watched his first wife run
off to become a vaudeville star, tried to create a circus

with a "Genuine White Elephant" as its star attraction. He had also been a freight hauler, a hotel owner, a partner in Woods Museum in Chicago, a theater owner and had failed as a business associate of Frank and Jesse James, two well-known bad guys.

In other words, Cap had more or less flopped in everything he touched. At age 50, about all he had was his old ringmaster's outfit—a green frock coat a couple of sizes too large for him—and a silk stovepipe hat. And he also had Ma, the former Maria Mulholland, who replaced Minnie, his first, vaudeville-loving wife. By all accounts, that was plenty, because Ma believed in standing by her man—except when she was drunk. Storytellers have described her as "a dipsomaniac, a rumpot whose periodic benders were epic. She would go off for a week at a time and all old Cap would say was, "It don't matter where she is. She's havin' a good time. She'll come home when she's ready." He was obviously a man who appreciated a good woman.

The turning point in Cap's life came shortly after he and Ma met a friend, Captain Bowen, who whispered that there was money to be made in Honduras. You see, he said, there's a revolution down there. So all you need to do is get there with a boat loaded with arms and they'll give you steamboat concession on the Honduras' rivers. You'd be rich.

So Cap immediately began to borrow, buy and build a boat. His ship, the Reutan, wasn't much, but Cap thought she'd make it. He wanted to test her and the best place to do so was on Lake Michigan during a storm. If the Reutan could stay afloat on that mean lake, it would surely survive the Gulf of Mexico.

On July 10, 1886, Cap, Ma, an engineer and four passengers set off into a gale. A miracle occurred. They actually made it to Milwaukee, where all the passengers refused the honor of making a round trip despite having tickets to do so.

While returning, despite being lashed to the helm, Cap was washed overboard seven times, with the powerful Ma hauling him back on board each time. Later, the engine broke down, but the engineer had lashed himself to his bunk and refused to budge.

The Reutan finally ground into a sandbar near the Chicago shore and there it stayed, its hull open in a dozen places.

But Cap wasn't defeated. He looked around and decided that this would be a fine place to live. The sandbar was only two or three inches below the water and it was rapidly growing around his boat. All he needed was a little more sand and he'd be on dry land. He offered local contractors the privilege of dumping anything they wanted near his home. Eventually, Cap even charged the builders for dumping.

He thus "created" 186 acres of land. That word, "created," is important. Cap Streeter found an old map of Chicago indicating that the shoreline ended to the west of his land. He claimed that he was beyond the shore of Chicago and Illinois, in his own district, the District of Lake Michigan. He recognized the laws of America, but of no other sovereign power.

In 1892, N. K. Fairbanks, who owned land opposite Cap's and who was a wealthy man, strolled over and demanded that Cap vacate. Fairbanks said, "I've got riparian rights."

Cap, waving his long-barrelled pistol, replied, "I got squatter's rights . . . and I got this."

Then, in a moment occasionally celebrated in story, song and on stage, Ma swooped into the scene and sliced off the heel of N.K. Fairbanks' boot with her trusty axe. It was as if she were vying for the honor of Wife of the Year. Her action started a war between Cap and the Chicago establishment.

Cap and Ma began throwing parties and, what's worse, selling booze on Sundays. That was against the law in Chicago, but Cap decided it was perfectly legal in his District.

His land, with its assorted outhouses, was an eyesore. The rich wanted him out of their front yards on the lake.

Some of Cap's more famous battles included:

• Summer, 1894—Five men from Chicago Title and Trust ordered Cap off his land. Cap grabbed his sawed-off musket, yelled, "You fellers git," and perforated their posteriors.

• Summer, 1894—Three policemen tried to arrest Cap for shooting at the five Title and Trust men. Ma poured boiling water on them, forcing them to retreat. Cap was later arrested, but the case was dismissed.

• Fall, 1894—Another attack, this time at 3 a.m., when Cap blasted all 25 invading policemen. Ma nearly

Cap Streeter's boat, 1893.

cut off the arm of one copper. Cap and Ma entered pleas
of self-defense and were released. Later, Cap discovered
a survey indicating that his "Deestrict" was outside the
city limits, so Cap named William H. Niles as his
military governor and began creating a separate state.

• Hoodlums surrounded Cap's Castle and were about
to destroy it, when they found his liquor supply. After a
long, riotous party, they were in turn surrounded by
Cap and his followers, who quickly wounded 35 of the
invaders. They were loaded into a cart and were taken

to the Chicago Av. police station, where Cap demanded that the invaders be charged with disturbing the peace, inciting to riot, breaking and entering, assault and trespassing. The police refused to press charges against a group of their own deputies.

• May 5, 1899—Cap created a courthouse in his outhouse, raised an American flag and issued his own Declaration of Independence. Cap and others were subsequently arrested, and released, on charges of illegal assembly.

• May 25, 1899—More than 500 hand-picked police officers (the number could have been anywhere from 100 to 1,000—stories about Cap tend to grow over the years) charged into the "Deestrict" because Cap allegedly shot at a police captain's buggy. Military Governor Niles responded by initiating trench warfare and by arming his men with old cannon grabbed from nearby parks. Cap didn't like this development because it hurt land values—he was selling lots in his Deestrict for as little as $1 or the price of a drink.

The city had Cap surrounded—a tug boat with a gatling gun was pointed at Cap's rear. The police charged, but were repulsed with buckshot and rocks, plus whatever was loaded into the cannons. Later, at nightfall, the police overwhelmed Cap Streeter and his group, but Cap was freed. The police were even reprimanded. After all, shooting at a Chicago policeman—or his buggy—wasn't a crime in those days.

• Police confiscated two of Cap's pistols after rummaging through his Castle while Cap and Ma were out. This led to one of Cap's most audacious moves.

Cap and Ma responded by going to the Chicago Avenue police station and holding everyone in the station as hostages. Yes, they held up a Chicago police station, as unbelievable as that sounds. They shoved a musket into the desk police captain's belly and got Cap's pistols back.

• Cap shot Samuel Avery in the seat of his pants. Cap's defense was so eloquent that he was acquitted.

• Spring, 1900—Men, posing as land buyers, burned Cap's home while he was away. Cap raised his own army, made an amphibious landing in Chicago, and then marched into Streeterville (or the Deestrict), taking it back.

In response, three-inch guns were mounted on two of the city's fire tugs, 16 patrol wagons were brought on line and over 400 policemen were used as reserve infantry. Later, a single policeman convinced Cap to allow himself to be arrested. He was, but he was also acquitted again of all charges.

• 1902—Cap and others indicted for forging President Grover Cleveland's name on a land grant which Cap used to prove that his Deestrict was outside the jurisdiction of Chicago. It was later reported that the document Cap used was actually a paper signed by President Martin Van Buren giving certain lands to John Kinzie and his heirs. The heirs immediately sued to get the land back, meaning that the rich people who were trying to get Cap off their beaches were suddenly defending themselves against a charge that they, too, were squatters.

• A mean Missouri gunman, John Kirk, was hired by

Cap Streeter, 1903.

local rich dudes in 1902 to put an end to Cap and his squatting. Kirk was found dead, with a bullet in his heart. And Cap was found guilty of the murder, despite his claim, "I never shot a man with anything but bird shot and everybody knows it." While Cap was in prison, Ma died. Then, after only nine months in jail, the governor freed Cap, granting him a full and unconditional pardon.

• A romantic interlude followed. When Cap was age 69, he married Alma Lockwood, age 36, in 1906.

• Throughout World War I, Cap continued serving beer and booze in his Deestrict, despite local laws against that, especially on Sundays. Cap said, "This here is a frontier town and it's got to go through its red-blooded youth. Streeterville won't never have a chamber of commerce until it has its cabaret. A church and a WCTU never growed a big town yet. You got to start with entertainment." That's been Chicago's convention philosophy ever since.

• About 1918—Cap was ordered to get a city liquor license. Cap stabbed the police sergeant carrying the order in the behind with a bayonet. Cap was arrested and was quickly bailed out.

• The next day eight policemen charged into the Deestrict. Two grabbed Alma's axe (or maybe it was Ma's axe which Alma inherited), while Detective Cudmore received "a scalp wound to the shoulder" (how's that possible?), probably from Cap's pistols. Alma claimed she had disarmed six policemen in the fray, and she was later arrested for assault with intent to kill. A local headline read, "CAP STREETER'S JOAN OF ARC REPELS THE BLUES." Alma convinced the court that any shooting had been accidental and that she didn't know her attackers were police. Cap and Alma were acquitted.

• Later that year, another case against Cap (we're not sure which one—there were so many) was thrown out of court because the judge said residents of Cap's District were not citizens of Cook County, the first judicial recognition of some of Cap's claims.

•Dec. 18, 1918—The day of defeat. The courts decided that Cap had no right to his land and he was finally evicted.

He began selling hot dogs and coffee at Navy Pier. He lost an eye when a sliver from some kindling he was chopping flew upward. This caused an infection and finally pneumonia. Cap Streeter died on Jan. 22, 1921. aboard his new houseboat, the Vamoose, docked off Navy Pier. He was 84 and the Mayor, plus half the city, went to his funeral.

The Vamoose became a menace to navigation and was destroyed by city order in 1928. Alma, who saved only Cap's musket as a momento (complete with bayonet), ended her days making and selling aprons. She died in 1936, age 66.

The final court case involving ownership of Streeterville was settled in 1940.

Cap's land extended from the Chicago River to Oak St. Beach east of Michigan Av. July 11, the day the Reutan was grounded, is sometimes Cap Streeter Day in Chicago, if local folks bother to remember the tobacco-chewing, gun-toting, birdshot-firing squatter. They should. His land, today, is easily worth $1 billion!

Chapter Seven: The Indians

" . . . raging sea of dusky,
painted, naked fiends . . . "
  John Dean Caton, 1835

Generally speaking, in Chicago—and American—
history the Indians have a terrible reputation. They
dance and whoop across the pages of most books,
painting themselves, making war, drinking and then
suddenly disappearing.

Unfortunately, the Indians didn't write down their
side of the matter. If they had, the white men who came
to Chicago would be pictured as invaders, who
whooped, danced, drank and made war; who stole
women, desecrated sacred areas, introduced diseases
and defrauded the Indian of land which rightfully
belonged to them.

Both pictures have some truth. Neither the Indian nor
the white man was blemish-free during pioneering days
and there were atrocities committed on both sides.

What follows are a few stories about the Indians and
their interactions with white settlers. The stories are
based on writings by white men and have a definite
white bias to them.

They are stories worth retelling because they are part

of our heritage. I apologize, in advance, for the fact that they are the white man's truth rather than the Indians' truth.

Pottawatomies, we'd know more about your side of the matter if a few of you had kept diaries!

THE DOOMED FORTRESS

The Indians' bad reputation in Chicago was made worse with the 1812 Fort Dearborn Massacre, a salvo in the British-American War of 1812. Perhaps it is time for a re-assessment. First, perhaps the massacre never had to occur. Second, the Indians were angry because the commander of the fort lied to them. Third, the "fort," despite being called "the best wooden garrison in the United States" at the time it was built, didn't offer much to praise by the time of the Massacre.

Fort Dearborn was named after one of the most inept leaders in American history. During the War of 1812, the Secretary of War Gen. Henry Dearborn took charge of all American forces from Lake Erie to the Atlantic. He then tried to capture Montreal, but he somehow never got across the Canadian-American border. Perhaps he couldn't find Canada.

Dearborn was finally fired by President Madison in 1813. Finis Farr in his book, *Chicago*, called Dearborn "one of the most ineffective leaders the nation has ever had to put up with." The man who narrowly avoided being court martialed left his name to a long and vital Chicago street, plus the ill-fated Fort and a variety of other Chicago parks and developments. He thus sets an example to us all as one of history's most successful failures.

The fort began when Capt. John Whistler, father of 15 children, arrived in Chicago on March 9, 1803, with a contingent of disgruntled troops, 60 per cent of which could not sign their own names. They spent the next few years drinking and deserting. Sometimes they hunted, such as the time a young soldier in a canoe spotted a deer swimming by him. He caught the deer and drowned it, an example of the rude pleasures available in the days before television reruns.

The fort was also entertained by the famous race between Capt. Whistler and a Pottawatomie chief. After both men bet their horses on the outcome, they ran five miles. Whistler won by a few yards. The two didn't meet again until the War of 1812, when the Indian, who was fighting for the British, challenged any American to individual combat. Whistler accepted the challenge and the two men hacked at each other with knives, swords and tomahawks until the Indian died.

The fort was beset with problems from the very beginning—half the men were sick the first year, Whistler had two fifers but their only fife was lost, and the first supply ship brought 56 suits of clothing for the captain's 66 men. It would be a chilly, embarrassing winter for at least 10 men in Fort Dearborn.

Things went from bad to worse when Whistler, who was the grandfather of James Abbott McNeil Whistler, the man who painted "Whistler's Mother," was replaced by Capt. Nathaniel Heald, the man some believe was a perfect military imbecile.

Concurrently, the military situation around the fort was deteriorating. By August, 1812, local Indians were wandering into the fort, picking up rifles and shooting them in Capt. Heald's parlor. It was obvious to everyone but Captain Heald that the neighborhood was going bad.

On Aug. 7, Winnemeg, or Catfish, a Pottawatomie chief, arrived with orders from Detroit to evacuate the fort. Then Catfish whispered to John Kinzie, a local trader, that the fort shouldn't be abandoned because it had ammunitions and provisions enough to withstand a six-month siege. Capt. Heald insisted on following orders, but not upon following them too quickly. He waited six days to make final arrangements and to make sure it didn't appear as if he was a coward who was fleeing the fort. He was attempting to save face, and the scalps of his men.

Then there was an Indian raid on Lee's Place, also called Hardscrabble, a short distance from the fort, on April 12. It was there that a corporal found a scalped Frenchman and another man who had been shot twice and stabbed 11 times in the chest.

After that, Heald held a council with the Indians, which his junior officers refused to attend. Later, the officers said that Heald's life was saved because they had a cannon trained in the group throughout the council.

Heald promised the Indians ammunition and food, plus other supplies, in return for safe passage. Both sides professed lots of good will and the council concluded.

The men of the fort were aghast. Give ammunition to

the Indians? That was like giving the fox a new set of teeth and letting him into the chicken coop.

Once back in the fort, Heald changed his mind and decided to get rid of the whiskey and "extra" ammunition. Others argued that, with what they were about to go through, there was no such thing as extra ammo, but Heald was undeterred. Barrels of whiskey were thrown into the river, which tasted like "strong grog" the next day.

And that only made matters worse. The Indians saw the firewater being spilled and were naturally upset. Black Partridge stopped by the fort to return his friendship medal and warned that he could not restrain the braves in his command.

After the blankets, broadcloths, calicos and paints were distributed to local Indians, there was the last-moment arrival of Capt. Billy Wells, leading 30 Miami Indians who were supposed to save the fort and Wells' niece, Rebekah, the wife of Capt. Heald.

But it was too late. The goods of the fort had either been distributed or destroyed. Capt. Heald ignored the fact that, with 17 barrels of salt and many live cattle, he could have slaughtered and preserved the meat for months and remained safely in the fort.

Despite near-insubordination by Heald's men, who thought his previous actions were "little short of madness," the gates to the fort were opened on Aug. 15, 1812. As the troops left, the band struck up the Death March. Capt. Wells had blackened his face, symbolic of the fate he fully expected. It was not the happiest parade ever seen on what was to become Michigan Ave.

About 500 Indians waited a mile and a half from the fort. The Indians began firing and the first trooper to fall was a 70-year-old man. The troops at Fort Dearborn were not the best of the front-line soldiers available to America.

Legend has it that during the massacre Wells was a great hero who deserved to have a Chicago street named after him. But legend must be tempered with a few facts at this point.

First, his 30 Miami Indians didn't do a thing during the battle. They refused to shoot fellow Indians and they went on their long rescue mission only to become spectators at the crucial moments.

Second, after Wells saw that the Indians were slaughtering the white women and children, he allegedly yelled, "Is that their game? Butchering women and children? Then I will kill, too." So he rode off to slaughter a few Indian women and children and was stopped by several Indians. It was not the most heroic quest ever undertaken.

His horse was killed. He was wounded, other Indians tried to save Wells, but Pee-so-Tum stabbed him in the back, killing him. Moments later, he was beheaded and his heart was torn out to be immediately eaten as a tribute to his bravery. The Indians of the time would not have gotten into the best restaurants.

Wells' last recorded words, spoken to his beloved niece Rebekah, was a message for his wife, "Tell her I died at my post, doing the best I could. There are seven red devils over there that I have killed." At least, that is what he was supposed to have said after taking an arrow in his lung, which is a mouthful, or a lungful.

The final score of those killed in action was: White people 43, Indians 15.

One kidnapped woman was immediately ransomed for 10 bottles of whiskey, although her Indian captor had to be assured that he would get the whiskey whether or not she died of her many arm wounds.

Another woman, Sgt. Holt's wife, grabbed her husband's sword and rode through the Indian lines wounding Indians as she went. The Indians chased her but didn't harm her because they wanted her horse. She hacked and sawed their rifle butts with her sword, as the Indians laughed and said, "The brave woman, do not hurt her." They finally grabbed her, showed her every kindness during her captivity and eventually returned her to her people. We do not know what happened to the horse.

Capt. Heald finally arranged a surrender to the Indians in exchange for the garrison's remaining lives. The Indians agreed, but later said the guarantees did not extend to the wounded, who were tortured for much of the night.

Many of the survivors later suffered terribly. Hugh Logan was tomahawked when he couldn't keep pace with the rest during the march away from the fort. August Mortt was killed that winter when he "went out of his head." One baby who cried too much during the march away from Fort Dearborn was tied to a tree and left to starve. William H. Hunt froze to death. Mrs.

John Simmons and her baby daughter were forced to run a gauntlet, which both survived—the daughter was the last survivor of the massacre and she died in 1900. Mrs. Isabella Cooper was pulled out of the wagon containing the women and children, and was actually scalped before being saved by a squaw. According to Milo Quaife's *Checagou*, Mrs. Cooper carried a silver-dollar-sized bald spot on her head for the rest of her life.

Perhaps the most pitiful survivor was James Corbin, who was shot in the hip, thigh and heel, and who had a tomahawk wound in his shoulder. He somehow lived through the long winter's months by crawling through the Indian camp searching for wood for a winter's fire and going for seven days at a time without food. He was eventually ransomed, and arrived in Quebec wearing only an Indian breechcloth and a ragged vest, with no shoes.

But according to Quaife, that didn't end Corbin's problems. He tried to get home to Virginia, but his discharge pay only got him to Albany, N.Y., where he faced starvation. He tried to re-enlist, but his wounds made him unfit for duty. He applied for a pension, but that was denied. Indians were supposed to kill their wounded prisoners and, since Corbin wasn't killed, he couldn't have been wounded at Fort Dearborn. It took him six long years to convince the government that it owed him a pension. But when it was finally granted, it amounted to only $4 a month!

Mrs. Kinzie was wounded in her arm, and the ball was extracted by her husband, who operated with a pen knife.

Capt. Heald was eventually freed, along with his wife. As he made his way to St. Joseph, Mich., word came to him that the Indians had changed their minds and wanted to recapture him. Still, the captain wasted an entire day in nearby Kankakee making arrangements for a more comfortable journey. Some folks just never learn.

It was four years before Fort Dearborn was reopened, and Capt. Hezekiah Bradley's first task was to bury the skeletons of those killed four years before. He didn't do a very good job of it because the sand in which they were buried along the lake front washed away and exposed the coffins in 1836.

By 1823, a visitor noted that Fort Dearborn had reverted to its old-fashioned ways. He wrote that "the village presents no cheering prospect . . . It consists of but a few huts inhabited by a miserable race of men, scarcely equal to the Indians from whom they are descended. Their log or bark houses are low, filthy and disgusting, displaying not the least trace of comfort."

Shows what can happen to a neighborhood bereft of a federal redevelopment plan.

MARRIED TO AN INDIAN XANTHIPPE

Sauganash was a Pottawatomie Indian chief who befriended the white men around Chicago. He was the son of an Irish colonel and a Pottawatomie woman, and he wrote in both French and English. He is credited with helping to convince other Indians not to join Blackhawk, a chief, when he went on the warpath in 1827.

Sauganash, who was known as Billy Caldwell, might have been successful in preventing war from spreading, but he failed at peace. He also tried to convince the Indians not to practice polygamy. However, they looked at Caldwell's own marriage to the daughter of an Indian chief. His wife's angry nagging was often heard coming from their wigwam during the still Chicago nights. The Indians would say that Sauganash was in favor of monogamy because he found one woman to be more than enough for him.

THE LAST WAR DANCE

The Chicago Indians' fling has seldom been equalled. That's no surprise. No one would like to live through that again!

However, it is fitting to end a chapter on the Indians by recalling the way they said good-bye to the white man.

On Sept. 28, 1833, a treaty was signed specifying that some 8,000 Chippewa, Ottowa, and Pottawatomie would give up all of their lands east of the Mississippi—some 5,000,000 acres—to be sold for less than two cents an acre.

Well, there were problems with the payments from the very beginning.

A down payment of about $150,000 worth of goods was made on Oct. 6, 1834. Local whites figured that, in exchange for a little whiskey, they could get all or most of those goods back from the Indians. So they ordered ships filled with whiskey to come to Chicago. Unfortunately or fortunately, depending on whose side you are on, a strong wind came up on Lake Michigan and no ships could arrive in Chicago for 16 days. It was written that "temperance men, philanthropists and Christians" rejoiced because of the gusts from heaven.

There wasn't much else to rejoice about when the 4,000 Indians gathered in a circle near Randolph and Canal Streets to get that payment. Halfbreeds and traitors were in the middle of the circle.

According to the Annual Review of 1853:

The crowd was so great around the pile of goods that those that were back from them could not get to them, and the outsiders at once commenced hurling into the air whatever missiles they could get hold of, literally filling the air and causing them to fall in the center where the crowd was most dense. There, to save a broken head, (they) rushed away, leaving a space for those who had hurled the missiles . . .

Several Indians were killed then and in the drunken brawl which followed.

The Indians said their final good-bye to Chicago on August 18, 1835. The treaty said they must move west at that time. Their exit would leave an indelible impression on the white man.

The dance began at the northeast corner of Rush and Kinzie. John Dean Caton, who would become the Chief Justice of the Illinois Supreme Court, wrote this vivid account of what happened.

. . . it was sort of a funeral ceremony of old associations and memories, and nothing was omitted to lend to it all the grandeur and solemnity possible. Truly I thought it an impressive scene of which it is quite impossible to give an adequate idea by words alone.

All were entirely naked, except for a strip of cloth around the loins. Their bodies were covered all over with a great variety of brilliant paints. On their faces, particularly, they seemed to have exhausted their art of hideous decoration. Foreheads, cheeks and noses were covered with curved stripes of red or vermillion, which were edged with black points, and gave the appearance of a horrid grin over the entire countenance. The long, coarse black hair was gathered with a profusion of hawk's and eagle's feathers, some strung together so as to extend down the back nearly to the ground.

They were principally armed with tomahawks and war clubs. They were led by what answered for a band of music, which created what may be termed a discordant din of hideous noises produced by beating on hollow vessels and striking sticks and clubs together. They advanced, not with a regular march, but a continued dance.

Their actual progress was quite slow. They proceeded up and along the bank of the river, on the north side, stopping in front of every house they passed, where they performed some extra exploits. They crossed the North Branch on the old bridge . . .in full view from the windows of the Sauganash Hotel . . . from which the best view of the dance was to be obtained, and these were filled with ladies as soon as the dance commenced. From this point of view, my own observations were principally made . . .

The morning was very warm, and the perspiration was pouring from them almost in streams. Their eyes were wild and bloodshot. Their countenances had assumed an expression of all the worst passions which can find a place in the breast of a savage—fierce anger, terrible hate, dire revenge, remorseless cruelty—all were expressed in their terrible features. Their muscles stood out in great hard knots, as if wrought to a tension which must burst them. Their tomahawks and clubs were thrown and brandished about in every direction, with the most terrible ferocity, and with a force and energy which could only result from the highest excitement, and with every step and every gesture they uttered the most frightful yells, in every imaginable key and note, though generally the highest and shrillest possible. The dance, which was ever continued, consisted of leaps and spasmodic steps, now forward and now back or sideways with the whole body distorted into every imaginable, unnatural position, most generally stooping forward, with the head and face thrown up, the back arched down, first one foot thrown far forward and then withdrawn, and the other similarly thrust out, frequently squatting quite to the ground, and all with a movement almost as quick as lightning. Their weapons were brandished as if they would slay a thousand enemies at every blow, while the yells and screams they uttered were broken up and multiplied and rendered all the more hideous by a rapid clapping of the mouth with the palm of the hand.

To see such an exhibition by a single individual would have been sufficient to excite a sense of fear in a person not overly nervous. A hundred such, all under the influence of the strongest and wildest excitement, constituting a raging sea of dusky, painted, naked fiends, presented a spectacle absolutely appalling.

When the head of the column had reached the front of the hotel, leaping, dancing, gesticulating and screaming while they looked up at the windows with hell itself depicted on their faces, at the 'chemokoman squaws,' with which they were filled, and brandishing their weapons as if they were about to make a real attack in deadly earnest, the rear was still on the other side of the river, two hundreds yards off; and all the intervening space, including the bridge and its approaches was covered with this raging savagery glistening in the sun, reeking with steamy sweat, fairly frothing at the mouths with unaffected rage, it seemed as if we had a picture of hell itself before us, and a carnival of the damned spirits there confined, whose pasttimes we may suppose should present some such scenes as this.

At this stage of the spectacle, I was interested to observe the effect it had upon the different ladies who occupied the windows almost within reach of the war clubs in the hands of the excited savages just below them. Most of them had become accustomed to the sight of the naked savages during the several weeks they had occupied the town, and had even seen them in the dance before, for several minor dances had been previously performed, but this far excelled in the horrid anything which they had previously witnessed. Others, however, had but just arrived in town, and had never seen an Indian before the last few days and knew nothing of our wild western Indians but what they had learned of their savage butcheries and tortures in legends and in histories. To those familiar with them, the scenes seemed actually appalling, and but a few stood it through and met the fierce glare of the savage eyes below them without shrieking.

It was a place to try the human nerves of even the stoutest, and all felt that one such sight was enough for a lifetime.

The question forced itself on even those who had seen them most: What if they should, in their maddened frenzy, turn this sham warfare into a real attack? How easy it would be for them to massacre us all, and leave not a living soul to tell the story.

Some such remark as this was often heard, and it was not strange if the cheeks of all paled at the thought of such a possibility. However, most of them stood it bravely and saw the sight to the very end; but I think all felt relieved when the last had disappeared around the corner as they passed down Lake Street, and only those horrid sounds which reached them told that the war dance was still progressing.

Chapter Eight: Culture

" . . . the feminine colossus who doth
bestride our operatic world . . . "
Written about Mary Garden, 1910

Chicago would probably be more comfortable about
"culture" if all artists also produced fine bowling shirts.

Today, ballet can be overwhelmingly popular in
Chicago, opera is sold out each season, the Chicago
symphony is among the best in the world, artists are
sometimes appreciated in their home town even though
the Art Institute does precious little to help local folks
make good, and playwrights can get started in Chicago,
as can comic actors, authors and others.

But there is always an ambivalence towards
"culture." In Chicago, ballet is still something sissies do,
opera is for Italians, theater is populated by hippies who
never bathe, and you better never let your daughter
marry an artist because he'll never support her.

Chicago is the home of real people who do real
things—fix cars, manufacture goods, mow lawns, have
kids, and play 16 inch softball. Art, theater, music and
dance are decidedly "unreal" because when they are
over, unless a movie or recording exists, they are gone.

You can't fondle them, as you would a golf trophy; and you can point with pride to them.

The following three stories about Chicago and "culture" show that the city can get quite involved in culture, but mainly when offered either something for nothing or when local sensibilities are attacked.

That still happens. Chicagoans have probably wasted more time pasting more electrical tape to hide more nude pictures in magazines and on marquees than the citizens of any other city in the world. And the results, aside from some steamy crusades and a bit of local aggravation, have been minimal.

At best, Chicagoans are slightly uncomfortable about "culture." At worst, they can produce hilarious and frustrating moments.

Possibly, Maybe, Allegedly the Biggest Swindle of the Season

We still do not know for sure whether or not the Great Lottery of Crosby's Opera House was a Big Fraud or a little gyp. We do know it was one of the great stories involving business and culture.

Uranus H. Crosby was an eminently successful distiller who bet that liquor prices would go up during the Civil War, who invested in large quantities of booze before the war and who became wealthy when America's wartime thirst was monumental. But he wanted to be known as more than a mere investor in liquor.

So Uranus Crosby built Crosby's Opera House in Chicago for between $600,000 and $700,000, an enormous sum. He would have his wealth and his palace of culture.

His Opera House, built of marble, included a 30- by 60-foot art gallery. Within the theater, there were 56 private box seats, a dome with portraits of Beethoven, Mozart, Auber, Weber, Verdi, Wagner, Gounod, Gluck, Bellini, Donizetti, Mayerbeer and Rossini, with a gilt ceiling, a 40-foot painting of "Aurora" over the orchestra and, on the parapet over the entrance, statues representing Painting, Sculpture, Music and, of all things, Commerce. "Commerce" has seldom been in finer company.

Writers called it the "finest public building in the West." However, it was ill-fated from the moment it was scheduled to open, on Monday, April 17, 1865.

That was not an auspicious day. Just two days before, on Saturday, April 15, 1865, President Abraham Lincoln was shot. The Crosby Opera House opening was postponed until that Thursday.

From that day forward, the Opera House was in trouble. "As a financial investment," wrote historian A. T. Andreas, "it was a failure."

Crosby, being a good businessman, decided to recoup his losses with a single, brilliant stroke. He would offer his Opera House, yes, the entire Opera House, in a lottery. For a mere $5, any rube anywhere might own the finest public building in the West, a $600,000 return on a $5 chance.

Furthermore, with each $5, the purchaser would also

get plates titled "Mercy's Dream" or "The Little Wanderer." That salved some consciences of those opposed to gambling, but in favor of "encouraging artistic tastes" (Andreas). It was said years later that such plates were hanging on parlor walls throughout the Western states and on dark closet walls, "while in every quarter of the land, private pocket-books were lightened of greenbacks."

The drawing was supposed to take place on Oct. 11, 1866, but it was postponed. In the meantime, many people visited Chicago and stopped by the Opera House, inspecting it as if they were already the owners.

Those who couldn't afford the $5 for a ticket formed investment clubs so that many could participate in the purchase of a single chance. The clubs included those named Scalpers Revenge, Bloody Tub, Deadbeat, Kiss Me Quick, Squeeze Me Tight, Bottom Dollar, Bohemian Club, and Dead Broke.

Excitement reached a fever pitch. One reporter wrote, "It was the most colossal event in Chicago's history between the Civil War and the Great Fire." And it would have a most mysterious ending.

On the day before the drawing the "city was taken by storm. It no longer belonged to itself," wrote the Chicago Republican newspaper.

Every train from every point of the compass came heavily laden with strangers, who, being unprovided with certificates, rushed to purchase them, and reappeared, after a time, furnished with engravings . . . . As a matter of fact, there were so many that it was utterly impossible to accommodate them. The hotels were filled. The Armory was filled. The saloons were filled . . . .

Where they all slept Sunday night—if they did sleep—who can say? Some roamed back and forth through the streets all night, stopping occasionally to take a little refreshment from the inevitable carpet-bag. Some sat on steps, and some on curbstones, and whistled. Some having insured warmth by a previous intoxication, laid themselves on the snow, and were still . . . .

The drawing was on Jan. 21, 1867. The Board of Trade was deserted. Only one courtroom in the city was hearing a single case. Shops were closed, and the city stopped, as the mob charged into the Opera House promptly at 11 a.m.

At that moment, again according to the Chicago Republican, "The crowd flung itself into the broad passage . . . Carpet-bags were torn from clasping hands and trampled under foot. Pictures were dropped and crushed. Coats were rent. Toes were trodden on, and hats sunk to rise no more. Men screamed and women fainted. Policemen swore and sergeants scolded . . . " Eventually the crowd took their seats.

Two wheels were brought on stage. The larger one contained the 210,000 tickets, including the 25,593 which Crosby kept for himself. No one complained about that. It seemed fair at the time. The smaller wheel had 302 tickets each representing a painting, vase or statue to be raffled off along with the Grand Prize of the entire Opera House. Of the 302 prizes, nine were judged to be quite valuable works of art.

As tickets were taken from each wheel, it became evident that Uranus H. Crosby was quite a lucky man. He won the second prize, a "masterpiece" worth $20,000 and titled "The Yosemite Valley"; the third prize, a $6,000 painting titled "An American Autumn"; the sixth prize, a painted titled "Recognition"; and an invaluable bust of Lincoln.

But it was the 113th ticket to be drawn which caused the most excitement. That was for the Opera House itself and it went to ticket number 58,600. No one stepped forward to claim the prize. No one shouted with joy. No one cried and hugged their neighbors. No one.

The drawings continued until all the prizes were given out, and then the city went wild with speculation. Many thought that Bock Meyer, a saloon owner, had won. When Crosby later visited Meyer's bar, while Meyer was out, Meyer's bartenders were sure the boss had won. So, according to historian Lloyd Wendt, they began setting up drinks for everyone on the house. They passed out seven free kegs of beer and gallons of whiskey before the irate owner arrived to stop the flow of booze. Meyer was supposed to have said, "Gott in Himmel! I don't even got a ticket on the place."

The Chicago Tribune, after fuming that Crosby took so many of the best prizes himself, reported, "It also turns out that the Opera House to be deeded is not the while building as represented but only the audience room in the inaccessible center of the block. If this proves the biggest swindle of the season, no one will pity the victims." The Tribune never did like gambling.

The winner, it was finally revealed, was an "A. H. Lee" of Prairie du Rocher, Ill. Some folks doubted the guy's existence. Reporters couldn't find any Colonel Abraham Hagerman Lee in Prairie du Rocher, which didn't have a telegraph office.

Three days later, a St. Louis newspaper printed a letter from Col. Lee to his brother-in-law. The letter said that Lee was tending to his sick wife when suddenly "the whole neighborhood was in an uproar."

Wealth did not come to A. H. Lee when he was dressed for the occasion. The letter noted, "I had undressed myself, as it was growing late, and was sitting in my long-tailed nightshirt, discussing the events of the evening, when a thundering knock at the door announced all was not over yet." A messenger arrived bearing the good news, but Lee said he couldn't leave his sick wife to take possession of the theater.

Lee finally, allegedly, reached Chicago on Jan. 25, where it was reported that he was a former riverboat pilot and Civil War veteran. He also supposedly said that he agreed to sell the Opera House back to Crosby for $200,000.

Figure it out. About $972,035 worth of chances were sold. The most Crosby claimed to have spent was $200,000 on "Lee," leaving him with a $700,000 profit! What if "Lee" were mere fiction and no payment of $200,000 were ever made? Crosby kept the Opera House, paid off all debts, and had a handsome profit, in exchange for giving away a few paintings.

One historian has written that a few reporters
actually talked to "Lee" when he was in Chicago. The
other writers claim that the only public contact with Lee
was via the letter to his brother-in-law published in St.
Louis and the letter to the Chicago Republican saying
that "Lee" got $200,000 from Crosby and left town
without meeting the folks because he didn't want to
"become the object of unpleasant notoriety."

As far as the principals of the drama were concerned,
"Lee" was supposed to have gone home and built a
mansion. Crosby had to leave town and went into exile
in New England. His brother took over the theater,
which later became the place where Republicans
gathered to nominate General Ulysses Grant for
President in 1868.

The theater had several more exciting moments in its
history. Edward Payson Weston walked from Portland,
Maine, to the theater to win a $10,000 bet that he would
walk the 1,237¾ miles in 26 "secular" days (30 days in
all). He did it, with time to spare, averaging 52 miles a
day, but covering 91-, 80- and 70-miles on his better
days. There were a lot of people betting against him and
he needed a large, tough police escort in Chicago to
make sure he completed the walk safely.

Lydia Thompson and her British Blondes appeared at
the Opera House in 1869 and 1870, leading Wilbur F.
Storey, publisher of the Chicago Times, to complain,
"Bawds in the Opera House! Where's the police?" Lydia
and her beefy ladies were the forerunners of burlesque
because they appeared in shocking tights.

Storey was outraged. He called Thompson's troupe

"large limbed, beefy specimens of a heavy class of British barmaid." He cried, "Opera has given way to burlesque. Music is routed by padded calves . . .and the glare of cheap tinsel."

Lydia got angry and settled things her own way. On Feb. 24, she approached Storey and began horse-whipping him, while his wife shouted, "Pull your pistol, Wilbur."

The Opera House had just one more act to perform. It was redecorated for $80,000, with a grand re-opening scheduled for Oct. 9, 1871, when a 60-member orchestra would play and the audience would hear piano, violin, coronet and harp solos. After the British Blondes, the theater would move to music by Beethoven, Schumann, Liszt, Wagner, Weber, Schubert, Gounod and Chopin.

However, according to Andreas, "That night the Demon of Desolation shook his smokey wings above those noble walls, and blew the fiery breath of fell destruction through the lofty pile. Gigantic in its conception, magnificent in the execution of its plan, monumental in its achievement, blurred with financial losses, yet rallying from them by an effort consistent with its general magnitude, the ending was like unto the beginning. As it was the greatest of its kind while existing there, so it was in its destruction swept away by the greatest flood of fire. Its end was absolute . . . "

In other words, Uranus Crobsy's Opera House was destroyed in the Chicago Fire of 1871 and was not rebuilt.

Looking back, Uranus might have succeeded if he had had more Lydia and less opera.

No One Attacks the Water Tower, Understand?

Chicagoans love their Water Tower, because it survived the fire of 1871, because it is old and because it is, well, lovable. So when "culture" attacks the Water Tower, look out.

That happened in 1882, when Oscar Wilde visited Chicago during a lecture tour. He was, at the time, a recognized homosexual, meaning he was fair game for the reporters of the day.

One said that Wilde shook hands like the "clinging of a vine." Another newspaper poetically thought:

Here in the energetic West
　We have no vacant niches
For clowns with pansies in the vest
　Or dadoes on the breeches.

So Wilde attacked the poor Water Tower, saying that the tower was "a castellated monstrosity with pepper boxes stuck all over it. I am amazed that any people could so abuse Gothic art and make a structure look not like a water tower but like a tower of a Medieval castle." He suggested that the Water Tower be torn down and that the entire city looks "positively dreary."

Chicago survived.

THE VIBRATIONS WERE ALL WRONG

The town was in an uproar and it was all Mary Garden's fault. There she was, in the staid Auditorium Theater, singing and slinky-dancing in "Salome."

The Chief of Police, Col. Leroy T. Seward, reviewed her 1910 performance as follows: "It was disgusting. Miss Garden wallowed around like a cat in a bed of catnip. There was no art in her dance that I could see. If the same show were produced on Halsted Street, the people would call it cheap, but over at the Auditorium, they say it's art. Black art, if art at all. I would not call it immoral. I would say it is disgusting."

"Salome" had three of its scheduled four performances before packed audiences. The reviewers called Mary Garden "the feminine colossus who doth bestride our operatic world" and thought her "Salome" was a "florid, excessive, unhampered tour de force, lawless and inhuman." However, Arthur Burrage Farwell, president of the Chicago Law and Order League, refused to go to the Auditorium, saying, "I am a normal man, but I would not trust myself to see a performance of 'Salome.' "

Amid the controversy, the fourth show was suddenly cancelled by Edith Rockefeller McCormick (See Chapter Nine: Lovers). According to Mary Garden's autobiography, Ms. Garden then appealed to Mrs. McCormick by saying, "I've given three performances of 'Salome' and you've occupied your box for each one of them. Why can't I give the fourth?"

Mrs. McCormick solemnly said, "It's you. The truth

came to me in a flash when I went home after your third performance . . . I said to myself, Edith, your vibrations are all wrong." And so, because of mis-tuned vibrations, "Salome" was cancelled.

However, Mary Garden also learned that famed preacher and former baseball player Billy Sunday was warning people about "Salome." Mary Garden confronted Billy Sunday after one of his sermons and the dialogue went like this:

GARDEN: What have you been preaching about me and "Salome"?

SUNDAY: I'm not going to tell you.

GARDEN: But I must know. I'm sure people are telling you lies about me. What have you said about "Salome," Mr. Sunday?

SUNDAY: Miss Garden, that's a very sinful opera.

GARDEN: Mr. Sunday, it's all in the way you take it. And now will you stop talking about me and have you got a drink of water.

That was, at least, the way Mary Garden remembered this odd confrontation. Instead of giving her water, Billy Sunday invited her to the nearest drug store to enoy a soda (a sundae would have given the story a certain poetic completion). After that, Sunday apologized to Miss Garden.

That was a better conclusion than what happened with Mary Garden's controversy with the Auditorium and Mrs. McCormick. Ms. Garden at one point said, "If there is any more of this twaddle about immorality, I shall leave Chicago and go to Philadelphia or some place where art is appreciated and viewed as art."

It was obviously the view of Chicago society, but not of Billy Sunday, that Mary Garden and her wallowing-in-a-bed-of-catnip dance could damn well go to Philadelphia!

Chapter Nine: Lovers

He covered "the natural beauty of
my wrists with the artificial
beauty of rubies, diamonds and
emeralds."
Ganna Walska

In April, 1979, Playboy Magazine concluded its survey
of "Sex in Chicago" with:

"More than any other single ingredient, Chicago sex
is fueled by money. No matter how a man looks or
makes his living, he's bound to have better luck if he's
upwardly mobile. Or, put simply: If you're looking for
sex in Chicago, you not only have to work *at* it, you
have to work *for* it. Only the flush survive."

Oddly enough, sex in Chicago, 1979, was about the
same as sex in Chicago, 1879. It is a town which uses
money as an aphrodisiac.

But sex and romance in Chicago can be two very different commodities. Chicagoans, who rhapsodize about
their lake front and their one or two days of nice spring
weather, are incurably romantic. There is no one in the
Chicago area who hasn't looked out at two feet of
blowing snow in mid-winter, before it has been dirtied
by bus exhausts, and who hasn't said, "It makes the city
look pretty, doesn't it?"

However, this chapter only includes stories about two Chicago romantics. Others can be found in chapters about Chicago's moguls, who could wax eloquent about the romance of money, or mayors, who could spin poetry about bringing in the votes.

Furthermore, Chicagoans seldom kiss and tell. The city's lovers aren't like the folks in Los Angeles, who often kiss, tell and show Polaroids or 16 mm. sound films of their adventures, or the good burghers of New York, who seem to kiss, tell and stab each other.

If all the great lovers of Chicago history were to gather in a single room, no one would say a word. There would be a lot of knowing smiles, a few nods of recognition and discreet, but rapid, exits.

The following two stories can be told mainly because the courts, our most unromantic institutions, intervened and demanded certain public disclosures.

CHECKING THE SPREAD OF IMMORALITY AMONG THE OLD AND DECREPIT

Chicagoans should have given Mrs. Leslie Carter a medal for entertaining them the way she did in April and May of 1889. Hers was the most celebrated divorce trial of an age of few divorces and she was probably the most famous Midwest lover of the late 1880s.

Eventually, Mrs. Carter was found guilty of adultery with Kyrle Bellew, while her husband was found innocent of all charges resulting when both sides sued for divorce.

She had been accused of having romances with D.S.

Gregory, State Sen. James F. Pierce (who sent her love poetry), Dr. J. B. Gilbert, William K. Constable (who gave her $60,000 so she could go to Europe) and Bellew (who gave her dramatic lessons). Attorneys said there were others, but they were confining their charges against her to those infidelities committed in America. They would not inconvenience any of her European admirers.

Thanks to the newspapers of the day, we are left with indelible descriptions of Mrs. Carter, who was the beauty of the age. For instance:

The Morning News, April 17, 1889: "She is decidedly an attractive woman of the blonde type. The lines in her face . . . indicate 30 years at least . . . Her poses have a langorous, sentimental air and her face suggests an ardent temperament rather than a weak will. Her hair is a breath of autumn sunset, neither yellow nor red, but pale auburn . . . Her full red lips show a smile that would make daisies blossom in a snowdrift in midwinter."

Afternoon News, April 16, 1889: "From her swelling bosom depended an oxidized silver scent bottle for use in case she should be compelled to faint. Her lips were red, like cleft strawberries, her eyes were soft and of the melting order, and her hair was as golden as the dandelions which dot the meadows on a fine spring day. It was not blonde under which come all colors from bright orange—falsely called 'red hair'—to the hue of dried hay. It was yellow—yellow as a sunflower, yellow as a buttercup, yellow as . . . yellow."

Chicago Tribune, April 17, 1889: "Promptly at 10 o'clock, fashionably attired in a rich, tight-fitting walking suit of black that showed her mature figure to excellent advantage, Mrs. Leslie Carter, the complainant, entered the courtroom escorted by one of her attorneys. A dainty hat of black, trimmed with a large showy ostrich plume was set coquettishly on her head. A wealth of golden hair struggled to free itself from bondage. To relieve the sombre black, she wore a tiny golden charm and an enamel violet upon which glistened a brilliant diamond. Through a filmy black veil, her complexion seemed matchless. One feature alone detracted from the beauty of the fair complainant— the mouth, with its red, strawberry lips looked too coarse for the fairer emotions . . . "

Chicago Times, April 16, 1889: "Her hair was the color of an August stubble field and her lips (were) red and inviting."

The trial dragged on until May 23, 1889, when the judge announced that "it is a case of national interest." The jury deliberated for 12½ hours.

Towards the end of April, the rule of courtroom procedure had to be changed. Before that, people under 35 were not admitted into the courtroom for fear that the steamy testimony might affect their morals. This meant that few women, who might not wish to admit they were over 35, witnessed the trial. On April 23, the judge announced that he didn't want his courtroom to replace the local burlesque houses. He added, "An old curiosity monger is quite as reprehensible as a young curiosity monger." The 35-year-old age limit was

Mrs. Leslie Carter in Maugham's play "The Circle," Chicago 1922.

rescinded, with the chief bailiff adding, "We must check the spread of immorality among the old and decrepit."

Eventually, Mrs. Carter was acquitted of all charges of adultery, except the one with Mr. Bellew, who was hissed while appearing on Chicago stages after the trial. Because of the notoriety of the trial, she met David Belasco, famed theater producer. Mrs. Carter became a stage sensation about five years later in such hits as "The Heart of Maryland," "Zaza" and "DuBarry."

Her husband, who won the case, lost his fortune, went insane and eventually killed himself.

Smiles which can make daisies bloom in a snowdrift in midwinter will sometimes do that to a man.

HAROLD LOVED GANNA, POLA, VIOLET AND TO WHOM IT MAY CONCERN

It may be that the saddest love story in Chicago history concerned Harold McCormick and Edith Rockefeller McCormick.

Edith loved Harold, but Harold loved opera singer Ganna Walska, his "protege" Betty Noble, actress Pola Negri and the Baroness Violete Beatrice von Wenner, who accompanied him on a harp during his whistling concerts.

Harold, it seems, was not lucky in love. He left Edith while he was in hot pursuit of Ganna, who unfortunately (for Harold) married Alexander Smith Cochran, billed as the world's richest bachelor.

Then, according to Emmett Dedmon's *Fabulous Chicago*, Cochran mightily offended the spiritual sensibilities of his grand diva. He made the unforgivable mistake of asking Ganna Walska to pick out anything she wanted from Cartier's and then he wrapped the eight or nine Cartier diamond bracelets she chose in "ugly looking rubber bands." Cochran then compounded his errors by giving Ganna a Rolls Royce, reserving entire floors of French hotels for her, sending her to the Rivera with half a dozen servants, giving her a sable coat which made her look "old and fat," and wanting to cover, her journal stated, "the natural beauty of (her) delicate wrists with the artificial beauty of rubies, diamonds and emeralds." The man was obviously an insensitive clod and deserved what he got— which was Ganna Walska, for a while.

He gave her $200,000 when they divorced, which was less than Dr. Joseph Fraenkel, her first husband, gave her on his death—about $500,000.

Meanwhile (and affairs of the heart do get complicated), McCormick had convinced the distraught and ever-loving Edith to grant him a divorce. He then went to Paris only to discover that Ganna and Cochran had married. So he had coffee with Ganna while Alexander slept on their wedding day.

It must have been quite a kaffeeklatsch because, when Ganna got her divorce, she agreed to marry Harold. Before that happened, Harold, a reaper heir, sent her one of every machine made by his company, International Harvester. It was difficult to know how Ganna would react to gifts. Diamonds and rubies made her angry, but she loved to see the army of threshers parading across her (actually Cochran's) lawn.

But McCormick wanted more than Ganna. He wanted the sex life of a teenager. So he got the Steinach operation, a rejuvenation process intended to bring back his sexual vigor. The operation, it was whispered, gave McCormick glands taken from a younger man. According to *An American Dynasty*, by John Tebbel, Harold's friends in bars in Chicago and New York created the following ditty to commemorate his operation:

Under the spreading chestnut tree
   The village smith stands.
The smith a gloomy man is he;
   McCormick has his glands.

McCormick married Ganna Walska, but the rejuvenated couple did not find happiness. Ganna noticed that Harold "idolized the physical expression of love." However, Ganna Walska saw herself, according to her journal, as "an idealist who was able to put so much value on the richness of his soul that she could not even imagine the possibility of his preferring to seek further for a gross and limited pleasure rather than being satisfied with the divine companionship of the spiritual love she was willing to share with him." In other words, Ganna was zip in the sack but was paired with a man who was constantly receiving encouragement from a younger man's glands. It would be fair to ask, "Could that marriage last?"

It couldn't. Harold and Ganna separated in 1931, with Ganna getting a fourth of his worth, or $6 million.

Edith, meanwhile, met Carl Gustav Jung, a Swiss

psychologist, decided that Chicago would become the psychological capital of the world, and began planning a dream city for millionaires, called Edithton, to be planted south of Kenosha, Wisc.

Harold continued to send Edith a single rose on her birthday. He rushed to her bedside when she died in 1932 and discovered that, through all the years, through all the Gannas, Betties, Polas and Violets, Edith Rockefeller McCormick had kept a room waiting for Harold in their Lake Shore Drive mansion in case he should ever want to return to her.

All of which must prove something. Perhaps it meant that the way to a woman's heart is ploughed with tractors rather than strewn with sables. Or avoid Polish opera stars unless you wish to whistle a sad tune. Or all the glands in Switzerland cannot bring happiness.

Afterthought

There are those who will say that the stories you have just read could not happen again, that they are about a time when the heroes were bigger, the scoundrels more outrageous and when fewer people quietly wore the three-piece corporate uniforms of today.

However, while this book was written:

The Chicago Sun-Times opened its own bar, The Mirage, and many city officials requested bribes of the undercover reporters there. After stories revealed widespread corruption, the earliest results were increases in the price of bribes in the city.

More than a third of the city's Bureau of Electrical Inspectors were indicted for extortion two days after four city building department supervisors were convicted for taking bribes.

Robert Quinn, the former fire chief, died in 1979. He ordered the air raid sirens to sound in 1959 when the White Sox won the pennant, scaring thousands of Chicagoans who were sure the Russians were then taking Lake Michigan. He promised, "If the White Sox ever win another pennant, I'll do it again," which may be one reason why the Sox haven't won a pennant since then. He ordered his men to be physically fit and had them run along the median strip of the Kennedy Expressway during rush hour, causing one of the worst traffic tie ups in Chicago history. When asked why there were so few black Chicago firemen, Quinn said, "They don't like heat and smoke." When asked why injured Chicagoans were being transported in unsafe Cadillac ambulances, rather than being treated at the scene by paramedics, Quinn said he thought that if a Chicagoan were going to die, he'd rather die in a Cadillac.

Mayor Michael Bilandic, seeking election in 1979, but troubled by the city's inability to get moving after a huge snowfall, compared criticism of his administration with the crucifixion of Jesus. He told Democratic precinct captains, "In the early history of Christianity, you see a leader starting with 12 disciples. They crucify the leader and made martyrs of the others. And what was the result? Christianity is bigger and stronger than it was before." It didn't work out that way. Bilandic and the Democratic machine lost in the biggest political upset of the decade.

Also in 1979, an angry woman, who looked as though she weighed less than 110 pounds sopping wet, whipped the best organized, richest, most entrenched and powerful city political machine in the country.

Chicago—it's still a frontier town.